SUBJECT CATALOGING DIVISION
PROCESSING SERVICES
LIBRARY OF CONGRESS

CLASSIFICATION
CLASS H
SUBCLASSES HM–HX

Social Sciences: Sociology

FOURTH EDITION

LIBRARY OF CONGRESS
WASHINGTON 1980

The additions and changes in Class H, Subclasses HM–HX adopted while this work was in press will be cumulated and printed in List 199 of LC Classification—Additions and Changes

Library of Congress Cataloging in Publication Data

United States. Library of Congress. Subject Cataloging Division.
Classification, class H.

Includes index.
Supt. of Docs. no.: LC 26.9:H/980
1. Classification—Books—Social sciences. 2. Classification—Books—Sociology. 3. Classification, Library of Congress. I. Title.
Z696.U5HM–HX 1980 025.4′6301 80–607033
ISBN 0–8444–0327–X

PREFACE

The first edition of Class H was published in 1910, with a second and fundamentally unchanged edition published in 1920. More than a quarter of a century was to pass before the appearance of the third edition in 1949, which incorporated developments during, between, and immediately after the two world wars. A reprint edition was published in 1967, which included supplementary pages of additions and changes made through 1964.

For the past ten years, the Subject Cataloging Division has wanted to issue a revised edition of Class H. However, the desire has been continually frustrated by the shortage of staff time to review the existing schedule, to propose badly-needed changes, to review and approve those proposals, and to prepare the new edition editorially. In 1977 the decision was made to publish another edition of Class H without fail, and catalogers began to review and prepare extensive revisions to the part of Class H devoted to economics. As work proceeded, it became clear that the study and review required to bring the entire schedule into alignment with current terminology and patterns of thinking while keeping up with regular work assignments were likely to prevent completion of the revision within a reasonable amount of time.

With oral support from librarians on the ALA RTSD CCS Subject Analysis Committee, it was, therefore, decided to follow an unusual course of action. It was previously decided that Class H would be published in two parts: H–HJ and HM–HX. However, the first part would represent a completely revised edition, whereas the second part would be merely an unrevised cumulation, incorporating changes made since the third edition, without any necessarily time-consuming attempt to update concepts and terminology. As a result, this edition of HM–HX, an unrevised cumulation, reflects the basic outline, tone and terminology of the early twentieth century during which it was developed.

Some changes have been made in this edition, primarily of an editorial nature. Lawrence Buzard, editor of classification, and Nancy Jones and Dorothy Thomas, assistant editors of classification, completed the cumulation, updating some terminology, arranging notes and references to conform to current practice, and deleting many parenthesized numbers. In addition, tables were arranged in a more consistent and uniform fashion reflecting the deletion of Cutter number countries from the tables at the end of the schedule. Many captions that can be recognized as obsolete have been reproduced as they appeared in earlier editions in order to enable this volume to be produced quickly and with a minimum of effort.

All legal materials now are classed in the appropriate subclasses of Class K that have been developed. Therefore, many numbers in HM–HK that formerly provided for laws and legal topics have been eliminated. However, some numbers relating to laws have been left in the schedule, as their removal would have caused time-consuming research. Any numbers relating to law should be ignored; current works are no longer classed there.

As of this writing, the revised edition of H–HJ is in preparation, with publication tentatively predicted in 1981. We expect to issue a revised edition of HM–HX as soon as practicable.

Mary K. D. Pietris, Chief
Subject Cataloging Division

Joseph H. Howard, Assistant Librarian
for Processing Services

SYNOPSIS

OUTLINE

HM		SOCIOLOGY (GENERAL)
	101-121	Civilization. Culture. Progress
	126	Unity. Solidarity
	131-134	Association. Mutuality. Social groups Including interpersonal relations, small groups
	136-146	Individualism. Differentiation. Struggle
	201-221	Social elements, forces, laws
	251-291	Social psychology Including public opinion, communication, crowds
HN		SOCIAL HISTORY AND CONDITIONS. SOCIAL PROBLEMS. SOCIAL REFORM
	30-40	The church and social problems
	41-46	Community centers. Social centers
	50-980	By region or country
HQ		THE FAMILY. MARRIAGE. WOMAN
	12-449	Sexual life
	19-30.7	Sexual behavior and attitudes. Sexuality
	31-64	Sex instruction and sexual ethics
	71-72	Sexual deviations
	75-76.8	Homosexuality. Lesbianism
	101-440.7	Prostitution
	450-471	Erotica. Pornography
	503-1064	The family. Marriage. Home
	750-755.5	Eugenics
	755.7-759.9	Parents. Parenthood Including parent and child, husbands, fathers, wives, mothers
	760-767.7	Family size. Birth control. Abortion
	767.8-792.2	Children. Child development Including child rearing, child life, play, socialization, children's rights
	793-799.2	Youth. Adolescence
	799.5-799.9	Young men and women
	800	Celibacy. Single women. Bachelors
	801-804	Courtship. Dating. Matrimonial bureaus. Trial marriage
	805	Desertion
	806	Adultery
	809-809.3	Family violence
	811-960.7	Divorce
	961-967	Free love
	981-997	Polygamy. Polyandry
	998-999	Illegitimacy. Unwed mothers
	1001-1048	The state and marriage
	1051-1057	The church and marriage
	1058-1058.5	Widows and widowers
	1060-1064	Aged. Gerontology (Social aspects). Retirement
	1075	Sex role
	1073-1073.5	Death. Dying
	1090	Men

HQ		THE FAMILY. MARRIAGE. WOMAN - Continued
	1101-2030.7	Women. Feminism
	1871-2030.7	Women's clubs
HS		SOCIETIES: SECRET, BENEVOLENT, ETC.
	101-330.7	Secret societies
	351-929	Freemasons
	951-1179	Odd Fellows
	1201-1350	Knights of Pythias
	1355	Other societies, A-Z
	1501-2460.7	Other societies. By classes
	1501-1510	Benevolent and "friendly" societies and mutual assessment fraternities
	1525-1560	Religious societies
	1601-2265	Race societies
	2301-2460.7	Political and "patriotic" societies
	2501-3365	Clubs Including boys' societies, Boy scouts, girls' societies
HT		COMMUNITIES. CLASSES. RACES
	51-65	Communities
	101-395	Urban groups. The city. Urban sociology
	161-165	Garden cities. "The city beautiful"
	165.5-169.9	City planning. Zoning
	170-178	Urban renewal. Urban redevelopment
	201-221	City population Including children in cities, immigration
	251-265	Mental and moral life
	321-325	The city as an economic factor. City promotion
	330-351	Metropolitan areas. Suburban cities and towns
	361-384	City and country. Growth of cities
	390-395	Regional planning
	401-485	Rural groups. Rural sociology
	601-1445	Classes
	621-635	Origin of social classes
	641-657	Classes arising from birth Including royalty, nobility, commons
	675-690	Classes arising from occupation. Middle class
	751-815	Serfdom
	851-1445	Slavery. Slave trade
	1501-1595	Races Including race as a social group and race relations in general
HV		SOCIAL PATHOLOGY. SOCIAL AND PUBLIC WELFARE. CRIMINOLOGY
	40-69	Charity organization and practice Including social case work, private and public relief, institutional care, rural social work, work relief
	70-72	State regulation of charities
	85-520.5	By region or country
	530	The church and charity

HV

SOCIAL PATHOLOGY. SOCIAL AND PUBLIC WELFARE. CRIMINOLOGY - Continued

541	Women and charity
544	Charity fairs
.5	International social work
553-639	Relief in case of disasters
560-583	Red Cross
600-639	Special types of disasters
640-645	Refugee problems. Refugee relief
650-670	Life saving
675-677	Prevention of accidents
680-694	Free professional services Including legal aid, medical charities
697-4959	Protection, assistance and relief
697-1493	Special classes. By age
697-700.7	Families. Mothers. Widow's pensions
701-1420.5	Children
835-844	Foundlings
851-859	Day nurseries. Foster day care
873-887	Destitute, neglected, and abandoned children. Aids and homes
888-907	Handicapped children
959-1420.5	Orphanages. Orphans
1421-1441	Young men and women
1442-1448	Women
1450-1493	Aged
1551-3024	Handicapped Including blind, deaf, mentally handicapped, physically handicapped
3025-3174	Special classes. By occupation
3025-3163	Seamen
3165-3173	Shop women, clerks, etc.
3174	Other. By occupation, A-Z
3176-3199	Special classes. By race or ethnic group
4005-4013	Immigrants
4023-4470.7	Poor in cities. Slums. Social settlements
4480-4630	Mendicancy. Vagabondism. Tramps
4701-4959	Protection of animals. Anti-vivisection
4961-4995	Degeneration
5001-5720.5	Alcoholism. Intemperance. Temperance reform
5725-5770	Tobacco habit
5800-5840	Drug habits. Drug abuse
6001-7220.5	Criminology
6035-6197	Criminal anthropology Including the criminal type, criminal psychology, prison psychology, causes of crime
6201-6249	Criminal classes
6250-6250.4	Victims of crimes. Victimology
6251-6773	Crimes and offenses
6774-7220.5	Crimes and criminal classes
7231-9920.5	Penology
7428	Social work with delinquents and criminals
7431	Prevention of crime, methods, etc.

OUTLINE

HV		SOCIAL PATHOLOGY. SOCIAL AND PUBLIC WELFARE. CRIMINOLOGY
	7231-9920.5	Penology - Continued
	7551-8280.7	Police. Detectives. Constabulary
	7935-8025	Administration and organization
	8031-8080	Police duty. Methods of protection
	8035-8069	Special classes of crimes, offenses and criminals
	8073-8079.55	Investigation of crimes. Examination and identification of prisoners
	8079.5-8079.55	Traffic control. Traffic accident investigation
	8081-8099	Private detectives. Detective bureaus
	8130-8280.7	Police: By region or country
	8290	Guards. Watchmen
	8301-9025	Prisons. Penitentiaries. Punishment and reform
	9051-9230.7	The juvenile offender. Juvenile delinquency. Reform schools, etc.
	9261-9430.7	Reformation and reclamation of adult prisoners
	9441-9920.5	By region or country
HX		SOCIALISM. COMMUNISM. ANARCHISM
	519-550	Communism/socialism in relation to special topics
	626-780.7	Communism: Utopian socialism, collective settlements
	806-811	Utopias. The ideal state
	821-970.7	Anarchism

Periodicals
Polyglot. American and English
1.A1-2 Polyglot
.A3-Z American and English
3 French
5 German
7 Other
9 Societies
Cf. H10+, Social sciences
13 Congresses
15 Collected works (nonserial)
17 Dictionaries. Encyclopedias
History
19 General works
22 By region or country, A-Z
Under each country:
.x General works
.x2 Biography, A-Z

Theory. Method. Relation to other subjects
24 General works
25 Relation to social works
Cf. HN29, Social surveys
HV40+, Charity organization and practice
26 Relation to philosophy
Cf. B63, Relation of philosophy to sociology
Relation to epistemology, see BD175
27 Relation to psychology
Cf. BF57, Relation of psychology to sociology
30 Relation to ethics
Cf. BJ51, Relation of ethics to sociology
Relation to religion, see BL60
Relation to education, see LC189+
33 Relation to politics
Cf. JA76, Relation of political science to sociology
Relation to communism/socialism, see HX542
34 Relation to law
Relation to international law, see JX1251
35 Relation to economics
Cf. HM211, Economic elements, forces, laws
36 Relation to history and geography
Cf. HM104, Historical sociology
.5 Relation to war
37 Relation to anthropology
Relation to science, see Q175.4+
Relation to art and literature
Relation to art, see N72.S6
Relation to literature, see PN51
Relation to linguistics, see P40+
Relation to leisure, see GV14.45
Museums. Exhibitions
41 General works
43 By region or country, A-Z
Under each country:
.x General works
.x2 Local, A-Z
Including special museums

Study and teaching
45 General works
47 By region or country, A-Z
Under each country:
.x General works
.x2 Local, A-Z
Including special schools
48 Research
General works, treatises, and advanced textbooks
51 English
55 French
57 German
59 Italian
61 Other European languages
62 Oriental languages, A-Z
63 Other languages, A-Z
Elementary textbooks
66 General works
68 Syllabi, outlines
73 General special
Civilization. Culture. Progress
Cf. CB, History of civilization
JC336, Social and evolutionary theories
101 General works
104 Historical sociology
Evolution. Biological sociology
106 General works
107 Anthropological sociology
108 General special
111 Degeneration
116 Mutation (Progressive principle)
121 Heredity (Conservative principle)
126 Unity. Solidarity
Association. Mutuality. Social groups
Cf. HM201+, Social elements, forces, laws
131 General works
132 Interpersonal relations
Cf. BF636, Applied psychology
BF637.C45, Interpersonal communication
RC488+, Group therapy
133 Small groups
134 Group relations training. T-groups
Individualism. Differentiation. Struggle
Cf. JC571+, Individualism (Political theory)
136 General works
141 The great man. Leadership. Prestige
Cf. BF412+, Genius
HX518.L4, Communist leadership
146 Equality
Social classes, see HT
Social elements, forces, laws
201 General works
Associative tendency, see HM131+
Environment. Regional sociology
206 General works
208 Physical elements, forces, laws
211 Economic
Cf. HM35, Relation of sociology to economics

Social elements, forces, laws - Continued

213 Intellectual

216 Moral

Including social justice, social ethics, etc.

219 Religious

221 Technological

Cf. CB478, Technology and civilization

T14, Philosophy of technology

T14.5, Impact of technology on modern society

Social psychology

Cf. HB849.44, Population psychology

251 General works

253 Sociometry

255 Instinct in social psychology

258 Communication

Cf. P87+, Communication (General)

261 Public opinion

263 Public relations. Publicity. Propaganda

267 Tradition

Authority and freedom

271 General works

276 Liberalism. Toleration

278 Passive resistance

Crowds. Tumults. Revolutions. Violence

Cf. RC569.5.V55, Psychopathology of violence

281 Theory

283 History

291 Other special, A-Z

299 Miscellaneous special

1 Periodicals. Societies. Serials
3 Congresses
5 Collected works (nonserial)
History
8 General
Ancient
9 General works
10 Special, A-Z
11 Medieval
Modern
General and early modern
13 General works
14 Social reform literature through 1800
19th century
15 General works
.5 Social reform literature
20th century
16 General works
17 Social reform literature
1945-
.5 General works
18 Social reform literature
19 Youth movement
25 Statistics. Social indicators
27 Essays, sketches, etc. (Descriptive)
For under each country, see HN57 and HN101-942.5, subdivision (5), (3), or (2)
Theory. Method. Relation to other subjects
28 General works
Relation to folklore, see GR42.5
29 Study and teaching. Research
The church and social problems
Cf. HV530, Church and charity
HV554.4, Church and disaster relief
HV645, Church and refugee problems
30 Periodicals. Societies. Serials
31 General works
32 Special other than local
Including social and problems in the mission field
For special by country, see HN61+, and HN101-942.5, subdivision (9) or (6) under each country
Religious denominations
35 Collective
37 Special denominations, A-Z
Class here general works only; for special regions or countries, see HN39
39 Special regions or countries, A-Z
40 Non-Christian sects, A-Z
.B8 Buddhists
.C6 Confucians
.H5 Hindus
.J3 Jains
.J5 Jews
.M6 Moslems. Muslims
Cf. BP134.S6, Social teachings of the Koran
Muslims, see .M6

Community centers. Social centers
Cf. GV51+, Recreation centers
HV4175+, Social settlements
LC215+, Schools as social centers
41 Periodicals. Societies. Serials
42 General works
By region or country
United States
43 General works
44 By state, A-W
45 By city, A-Z
46 Other regions or countries, A-Z
49 Special topics (not otherwise provided for), A-Z
.C6 Community development
.D3 Daylight saving
.P6 Power mechanics
.P8 The press and social reform
Cf. PN4888.C6, Corruption of the press
.V64 Voluntarism (General)
.W6 Women in social reform
By region or country
50 America
United States
51 Periodicals. Societies. Serials
52 Yearbooks. Directories
53 Congresses. By date
Associations (General)
Cf. H10+, Social sciences
HM9, Sociology
JS302+, Civic reform associations
54 Early to 1860/80
55 1860/80-
56 Documents
History and description
57 General works
58 1945-
59 1960-
60 Statistics. Social indicators
Social reform literature
Cf. HD6959+, Industrial relations
61 Early through 1800
64 1801-1945
65 1945-
Social ideals in literature, see PN51, PN1081, PN1643, etc.
78 Curiosa
Local
79 By region or state, A-W
Subarranged like HC107
Under each state:
.x General works
.x2 By county, parish, or regions, A-Z
.x3 Special topics (not otherwise provided for), A-Z
For classification by place, see .x2 or HN80
For topics, see subdivision (20), (10.Z9), or (5.2) in table on page 6

By region or country
  United States
    Local - Continued
80 By city, A-Z
      Including local associations
      In case of doubt, see JS
    Popular discussion. "Open forums"
83 General works
85 Special institutions, A-Z
90 Special topics (not otherwise provided for), A-Z
      For topics, see subdivision (20), (10.Z9) or (5.2) in table below
101-942.5 Other regions or countries. Table VIII, modified 1/
    Cf. HX101+, Socialism
    Under each country:

20 nos.	10 nos.	5 nos.	
(1)	(1)	(1)	Periodicals
(2)	.Z2-29		Yearbooks. Directories
(3)	(2)		Congresses
(4)			Societies
(4.5)	(2.5)		Documents
(5)	(3)	(2)	History and description
(5.5)	(3.5)	(2.5)	1945-
(6)	(4)	(2.7)	Statistics. Social indicators
		(3)	Social reform literature
(8)	(5)		Early through 1850
			.A1A-Z Periodicals
(9)	(6)	(3.2)	1851-1945
(10)	(7)	(3.5)	1945-
			Social ideals in literature, see PN51, PN1081, PN1643, etc.
(17)	(9)		Curiosa
(18)	(10)	(4)	Local, A-Z
			Including local associations
(19)		(5)	Popular discussion. "Open forums"
.A2	.Z4	.A2	General works
.A3-Z	.Z5A-Z	.A3-Z	Special institutions
(20)	(10.Z9)	(5.2)	Special topics (not otherwise provided for), A-Z
			.C6 Community development
			.E4 Elite
			.M26 Marginality, Social
			.M3 Mass media
			.M6 Moral conditions
			.P57 Polarization
			.P6 Power
			.P8 Public opinion
			.R3 Radicalism
			.S6 Social classes
			.S65 Social mobility
			.T5 Time allocation surveys
			.V5 Violence
			Cf. RC569.5.V55, Psychopathology
			.V64 Voluntarism

1/ For Table VIII, see pp. 135-144. Add country number in table to 100

By region or country

101-942.5 Other regions or countries. Table VIII 1/

Under each country: - Continued

2 nos.	1 no.	
(1)		General
	.A1-3	Documents
	.A4-6	Periodicals. Societies
	.A7A-Z	Yearbooks. Directories. Congresses
	.A8A-Z	History and description
	.A85A-Z	Statistics. Social indicators
(2)	.A9-Z8	Local, A-Z
	.Z9A-Z	Special topics (not otherwise provided for), A-Z For topics, see subdivision (20), (10.Z9) or (5.2) in table on page 6

Note 1: Pacific Islands

Under each, unless otherwise provided for:

.x General works

.x2 Local, A-Z

931 General

American possessions

932 General works

933 Hawaii

934 Other, A-Z

935-936 British possessions

937-938 French possessions

939-940 German possessions (Former)

Note 2: Poland

539 Local, A-Z

.5 Special topics, A-Z

For topics, see subdivision (20), (10.Z9) or (5.2) in table on page 6

960 Communist countries

980 Underdeveloped areas

1/ For Table VIII, see pp. 135-144. Add country number in table to 100

CF. GT2400+, Manners and customs

1 Periodicals. Serials
3 Societies
Including social hygiene associations
5 Collected works (nonserial)
7 Congresses
9 Dictionaries. Encyclopedias
10 Study and teaching. Family life education
Including marriage counseling
For manuals of marriage advice, see HQ734+
Sexual life
History. Sex customs
Cf. GN479.65+, Sex roles (Ethnology)
GR462, Folklore of sex
GT2600+, Love, courtship, betrothal, marriage (Manners and customs)
12 General
By period
13 Ancient
14 Middle Ages
15 Renaissance
16 Modern
18 By region or country, A-Z
Including general works on adults; for classification by sex, age or other special groups, see HQ27+
Biography of sexologists
.3 Collective
.32 Individual, A-Z
Sexual behavior and attitudes. Sexuality
Cf. HQ1075, Sex role
For general descriptive works on behavior in specific countries, see HQ18
For general works not by country, see HQ19+
General
19 Early works through 1800
21 1801-
Cf. BF575.L8, Love
BF692, Sex psychology
23 General special (Special aspects of the subject as a whole)
25 Curiosa
By sex, age, or other special groups
Cf. HV8836, Sexual behavior of prisoners
UH630, Sexual behavior of soldiers
Children, see HQ784.S45
Adolescents and young adults
27 General works
.3 Boys
.5 Girls
Adults, see HQ18
28 Men
29 Women
30 Aged
.5 Handicapped
.7 The sick

Sexual life - Continued

Sex instruction and sexual ethics

Cf. HQ728+, Treatises on marriage
RA788, Sex hygiene

31 Practical works. Popular manuals. Scientific treatises

32 Sexual ethics

For practical and ethical works, see HQ31

34 Textbooks for use in secondary schools

For juvenile textbooks, see HQ53

Works for special groups. By age, sex, etc.

35 Adolescents

.2 College students

36 Men

Cf. RC875+, Diseases of genital organs

41 Boys

46 Women

Cf. RG121, Female sex hygiene

51 Girls

53 Children. Juvenile works

54 Handicapped adults

55 Aged

Sex teaching

56 General works

57 Works for parents on teaching children

.2 Works on teaching special classes of children (not A-Z)

Sex instruction in the schools

Including curricula

For textbooks, see HQ34, HQ53

.3 General works

By region or country

.5 United States

.A3A-Z General works

.A4-W By state

.6 Other regions or countries, A-Z

58 The medical profession and sex teaching

59 The church and sex teaching

60 Sex research

61 Love and religion. Religious emotion and eroticism

Cf. BL65.S4, Sex and religion
BL460, Sex worship
BM720.S4, Sex (Judaism)
BS680.S5, Sex in the Bible

63 Sex relations and the church

Cf. BT708, Sex (Theology)
HQ1051+, The church and marriage

64 Other miscellaneous aspects. Esoteric theories

Sexual deviations

Including sex crimes

Cf. RC556+, Psychiatric aspects

71 General works. Psychopathia sexualis, etc.

72 By region or country, A-Z

74 Bisexuality

Sexual life - Continued
Homosexuality. Lesbianism
75 Periodicals. Societies. Serials
.2 Biography (Collective)
Lesbians
Biography
.3 Collective
.4 Individual, A-Z
.5 General works
.6 By region or country, A-Z
Male homosexuals
Biography
.7 Collective
.8 Individual, A-Z
76 General works
.2 By region or country, A-Z
.25 General works
.3 By region or country, A-Z
Gay Liberation Movement. Homophile Movement
.5 General works
.8 By region or country, A-Z
77 Transvestism
79 Sadism. Masochism. Fetishism, etc.
Prostitution
101 Periodicals. Societies. Serials
103 Congresses
106 Associations
General works. History
111 General
113 Ancient
Modern
115 General works
117 19th-20th centuries
120 Drugs and prostitutes
Regulation
121 General works
125 By region or country, A-Z
141-270.7 By region or country. Table V 1/
Under each country:

4 nos.

(1)	Documents
(2)	General works
(3)	By state, A-W
(4)	By city, A-Z

1 no.

	Documents
.A1-2	Serial
.A3-4	Monograph
.A5A-Z	General works
.A6-Z	Local

1/ For Table V, see pp. 135-144. Add country number in table to 140

Sexual life
Prostitution - Continued
Traffic in women
280 Periodicals. Societies. Serials
e. g. International Congress for the Suppression of the White Slave Traffic
Cf. HQ103, Congresses
281 General works
285 Cases, A-Z
Social purity
291 General works
293 General special. Prophylaxis
e. g. Morrow, Social diseases and marriage
295 The White cross
Rescue work
301 Periodicals. Societies. Serials
306 General works
311-440.7 By region or country. Table V 1/
Including local institutions
Under each country:

4 nos.
(1) Documents
(2) General works
(3) By state, A-W
(4) By city, A-Z

1 no.
Documents
.A1-2 Serial
.A3-4 Monograph
.A5A-Z General works
.A6A-Z Local

Girdles of chastity, see GT2810
447 Masturbation
449 Emasculation. Eunuchs, etc.
Erotica
Cf. PN6110.L6, Love
PN6233+, Anacreontic literature
450 Periodicals. Societies. Serial
451 Dictionaries. Encyclopedias
454 Anthologies, epigrams, etc.
458 History
460 General works
Literature
461 Early through 1800
1801-
462 English
463 French
464 German
466 Italian
467 Scandinavian
468 Slavic
469 Spanish. Portuguese
470 Other languages, A-Z
471 Pornography. Obscene literature
Cf. HV6727, Social pathology

1/ For Table V, see pp. 135-144. Add country number in table to 310

<u>The family. Marriage. Home</u>
Including kinship
History
503 General works
504 Primitive. Origins
Cf. GN480+, The family among savages
Ancient
505 General works
506 Assyria-Babylonia
507 Hebrews
508 Arabia
509 Egypt
510 Greece
511 Rome
512 Other (Celtic, Germanic, etc.)
513 Medieval
Modern
515 General works
518 19th-20th centuries
525 By race, nationality, or religion too broad for any one country, A-Z
.D78 Druses
.I8 Islam
.J4 Jews
531-727 By region or country. Table II 1/
Including marriage reform
Under each country:

2 nos.	1 no.	
(1)	.A1-4	History
(2)	.A5-Z	Other works

Treatises
Cf. HQ799.2.M3, Teenage marriage
General
728 Scientific
Other. Popular, the home, etc.
731 Early works through 1800
1801-
734 English
737 French
739 German
741 Italian
743 Other
745 Wedding ceremonies, forms, etc.
746 Bridal gift books
"Family records," <u>see</u> CS24
<u>Eugenics</u>
Cf. GN247+, Physical anthropology
RB155, Genetic counseling
Periodicals. Societies. Serials
750.A1A-Z Scientific
.A2A-Z Popular
.A3A-Z Congresses
.A4-Z Exhibitions

1/ For Table II, <u>see</u> pp. 135-144. Add country number in table to 530

	The family. Marriage. Home
	Eugenics - Continued
751	General works
755	Popular works. Guidebooks for parents
.3	Moral and religious aspects of eugenics
.35	Heredity and social problems
	Cf. HV4961+, Degeneration
.4	Eugenics and state. State policy (General)
.5	By region or country, A-Z
	Parents. Parenthood
	Including obligations, social role, rewards, desirability of children, etc.
.7	Study and teaching. Parent education
	Class here works on methods of instruction, educational programs, etc. For works on subjects taught, see the subject, e. g. HQ763+, Family planning; HQ768+, Child rearing
.8	General works
.83	Parental attitudes
.85	Relationship between parent and child
	Cf. BF723.P25, Psychological aspects
	Husbands. Fathers
756	General works
.5	Father's Day
	Stepfathers, see HQ777.7
	Wives. Mothers
	Cf. HD6055, Working mothers
759	General works
.2	Mother's Day
	Stepmothers, see HQ777.7
.4	Adolescent mothers
.6	Executive's wives
	Army wives, see U750+
.7	Foster parents
	Cf. HV875, Adoption
.9	Grandparents
	Family size
760	General works
761	Artificial insemination
	Cf. RG134, Gynecology
	Family planning. Birth control
	Cf. GN482.4, Ethnology HB875, Neomalthusianism RG136+, Gynecology
763	Periodicals. Societies. Serials
	Study and teaching. Research
.5	General works
.6	By region or country, A-Z
	Biography
764.A2A-Z	Collective
.A3-Z	Individual, A-Z
766	General works

The family. Marriage. Home
Family size
Family planning. Birth control - Continued
Moral and religious aspects
766.2 General works
Individual religions or denominations
.3 Roman Catholic Church
.35 Protestant churches
.37 Islam
.4 Other, A-Z
.5 By region or country, A-Z
.7 Population control (General)
For population control in individual countries, see HQ766.5
Abortion
Cf. HV6537+, Infanticide
RG734, Gynecology
767 General works
.3 Moral and religious aspects
.4 Abortion counseling
.5 By region or country, A-Z
.7 Sterilization
Children. Child development
Including the sociology of childhood
Class here comprehensive works on child development which emphasize social growth of the child; for works on child development which stress mainly the child's physical and psychological growth, see RJ131
Cf. GT2450+, Customs of children
HQ783, Socialization
HV701+, Child welfare
.8 Periodicals. Societies. Serials
.82 Congresses
.84 Dictionaries. Encyclopedias
.85 Study and teaching. Research
.87 History
.9 General works
Pictorial works, see HQ781.5
By region or country, see HQ792
Child rearing
Including care, training, character building, etc.
Cf. HV959+, Institutional care
LB1027.5+, Guidance and counseling in schools
LB1140+, Preschool education. Nursery schools
LC37+, Home education
RJ101+, Health and physical care
RJ206+, Nutrition and feeding
TX361.C5, Children's diets
768 Periodicals. Societies. Serials
Study and teaching. Research, see HQ755.7
769 General works
.5 Guidebooks for baby-sitters
Biography
.9 Collective
770 Individual, A-Z
.4 Disciplining
.5 Toilet training
.7 Safety training

The family. Marriage. Home
Children. Child development
Child rearing - Continued
Child psychology for parents (General)
Including guidebooks for parents on understanding children and their behavior
Cf. BF721+, Child psychology (General)
LB1101+, Child psychology for teachers
RJ111, Mental hygiene of children
For special topics in child psychology, including guidebooks for parents on these topics, see the topic, e. g. BF723.J4, Jealousy; LB1139.E5, RJ499, Emotionally disturbed children
771 Periodicals. Societies. Serials
772 General works
.5 Problems of children from the standpoint of the child
Rearing of special categories of children
Cf. BF723, Psychological aspects
LC3950+, Exceptional children
773 Problem children
Cf. BF723.E598, Child psychology
HV9051+, Juvenile delinquency
RJ499+, Mental disorders of children
.5 Gifted children. Exceptional children
Handicapped children
.6 General works
.7 Retarded children
774 Infants
.5 Preschoolers
775 Boys
777 Girls
Foster children, see HV875
.3 Only child
.35 Twins
Orphans, see HV959+
Adopted children, see HV875
Children in single parent families
.4 General works
.5 Children of divorced parents
.6 Children of working mothers
Cf. HV851+, Day care nurseries
.7 Stepchildren
Diaries
779 Babies. Baby books
.5 Children
Child life (Descriptive). Activities of childhood
Cf. GT2450+, Customs of children
HT206, Children in cities
HT453, Children in rural areas
781 General works
.5 Pictorial works
782 Play as a childhood activity
Including the social importance of play
Cf. BF717, Psychology of play
GV182.9, Guides for play
LB1137, Psychology of play for teachers. Education through play

The family. Marriage. Home
Children. Child development
Child life (Descriptive). Activities of childhood - Continued

783 Socialization. Social learning
784 Other special aspects, A-Z
.A34 Aged, Relations with
Brothers and sisters, Relations with see BF723.S43
.C6 Comic books, strips, etc.
Cf. HV9076.5, Juvenile delinquency
Communication, see BF723.C57
Conduct of life, see BJ1631+
Death, see BF723.D3
.E3 Eating habits
Employment, see HD6228+
.F5 Finger-sucking
.F7 Friendship
.G45 Geographical perception
Home activities, see HQ781+
.M3 Mass media
Motion pictures and children, see PN1995.9.C45
.N3 Nail biting
.N4 Newspaper reading
.N8 Nursery equipment
Oral communication, see BF723.C57
Parents, Relations with, see HQ755.85
Performing arts and children, see PN1590.C45
.P5 Politics
.Q4 Children's questions and answers
.R3 Radio
.S4 Saving and thrift
Security, see BF723.S22
Self-reliance, see BF723.S29
Sex interest, see BF723.S4
.S45 Sexual behavior
Cf. BF723.S4, Psychology
.S65 Stealing
.S8 Strangers, Relations with
.T4 Television
War, see BF723.W3
.W6 Work, Attitude toward

Children's rights. The child and state
Including protection of minors
789.A3A-Z Early works through 1800
.A5-Z General works
792 Social conditions of children. By region or country, A-Z
.2 Underdeveloped areas

Youth. Adolescence
793 International societies, congresses, collections, etc.
General, and United States
796 Both sexes
797 Male
798 Female
Cf. HQ759.4, Adolescent mothers

The family. Marriage. Home
Youth. Adolescence - Continued
799 Other regions or countries, A-Z
Under each country:
.x General works
.x2 Local, A-Z
e. g. .N4 Near East
.2 Special topics, A-Z
.D7 Dropouts
Cf. HD6270+, Youth labor
LC142, Attendance in school
Drugs and youth, see HV5824.Y68
.E7 Erotica
.M3 Marriage, Teenage
Cf. HQ759.4, Adolescent mothers
.M35 Mass media
.P6 Political activity
Sex relations, see HQ35
Socialism, see HX547
.T4 Television
Young men and women
.5 General works
.6 Young men
For young women, see HQ1229
By region or country
United States
.7 General works
.72 By state, A-W
.73 By city, A-Z
.8 Other regions or countries, A-Z
Under each country:
.x General works
.x2 Local, A-Z
.9 Special topics, A-Z
Drugs and young men, see HV5824.Y67
.P6 Political activity
800 Celibacy. Single women. Bachelors
For celibacy of the clergy, see BV4390
.2 Maiden aunt
Courtship. Dating
Historic courtships. "Great lovers"
801.A2A-Z Collections
.A3-Z Special
.A5-Z Popular works. Lovers' manuals
Cf. HQ25, Curiosa
Love letters. Letter writers
For literary collections, see PN6140.L7, PQ1288.L8, PR1349.L8, etc.
.3 English
.5 Other
802 Matrimonial bureaus. Marriage brokerage
.5 Matrimonial advertisements
803 Trial marriage. Companionate marriage
804 Breach of promise
805 Desertion

The family. Marriage. Home - Continued

806 Adultery

Family violence

Cf. HV6626, Wife beating

809 General works

.3 By region or country, A-Z

Divorce

811 History

General works

813 Early to 1800

1800-

814 English

815 French

816 German

817 Italian

818 Spanish

819 Other

820 The state and divorce

Divorce in international law, see JX6419

The church and divorce

For special denominations, see BX

823 General works

824 The Bible and divorce

831-960.7 By region or country. Table V 1/

Under each country:

4 nos.	1 no.	
(1)	.A2-29	Documents
	.A3	Special
(2).A6-Z	.A5-Z5	General works
(3)	.Z6	By state, A-W
(4)	.Z8	By city, A-Z

Free love

961 History

964 Literature

Particular communities

Cf. HX651+, Communism

967 By region or country, A-Z

Under each country:

.x General works

.x2 Local, A-Z

Polygamy

Cf. GN480.33+, Anthropology

981 History

Literature

987 Early

988 Modern

991 Bible and polygamy

992 Missions and polygamy

1/ For Table V, see pp. 135-144. Add country number in table to 830

The family. Marriage. Home

Polygamy - Continued

Polygamous sects

994 Mormons

996 Other, A-Z

997 Polyandry

Cf. GN480.36, Anthropology

Illegitimacy. Unmarried mothers

Cf. HV700.5, Protection, assistance, and relief (Unmarried mothers)

998 General works

999 By region or country, A-Z

For statistics, see HB903.I6

The state and marriage

1001 General works

1006 Civil marriage

1026 Consanguineous marriages

Cf. HV4981, Social pathology

1028 Marriage with deceased wife's sister

1031 Mixed marriages

Including material on mixed marriages in general

Cf. GN254, Racial crossing

HQ750+, Eugenics

Marriage of handicapped persons

1036 General works

1038 Blind

1040 Deaf

1041 Mentally handicapped

1043 Other

The church and marriage

1051 General works

1053 Catechisms

1057 The Bible and marriage

Widows and widowers

1058 General works

.5 By region or country, A-Z

Aged. Gerontology (Social aspects). Retirement

Including the middle aged

Cf. BJ1691, Ethics

BV4580, Religious life

GV184, Recreation

GV197.A34, Camps

HD6279+, Employment

HD7101+, Public medical care plans

HD7105+, Social insurance

HD7287.9+, Housing for the aged

HG9426+, Annuities

RA413.7.A4, Private medical care plans

RC952+, Geriatrics

1060 Periodicals. Societies. Serials

.5 Biography (Collective)

1061 General works

The family. Marriage. Home
Aged. Gerontology (Social aspects).
Retirement - Continued
Retirement
1062 General works
1063 Places of retirement
.5 Transportation
1064 By region or country, A-Z
United States may be subdivided:
.U5 General works
.U6 By state, A-W
Death. Dying
Cf. BD443.8+, Philosophy
BF789.D4, Psychology
BJ1469, Ethics
GT3150+, Burial customs
HD9999.U5, Funerals
R726, Euthanasia
R726.8, Terminal care
1073 General works
.5 By region or country, A-Z

1075 Sex role
Cf. BF692.2+, Psychology
GN479.65+, Ethnology

1090 Men

Women. Feminism
Cf. GT2520+, Customs relating to women
Periodicals. Societies. Serials
1101 English
1102 French
1103 German
1104 Other
1105 Yearbooks (International)
1106 Congresses
Collections
1111 General works
Anthologies, etc., see PN
1115 Dictionaries. Encyclopedias
History
1121 General works
1122 General special
1123 Biography (Collective)
.A2 Early works to 1800
Ancient
Including primitive
1127 General works
1130 Indo-Iranian
1132 Hebrews
1134 Greece
1136 Rome
1137 Other, A-Z
1139 Amazons

Women. Feminism
History - Continued
Medieval
1143 General works
1147 By region or country, A-Z
Renaissance
1148 General works
1149 By region or country, A-Z
Modern
1150 General works
1154 19th-20th centuries. Emancipation of women
Cf. HQ1423+ and HQ1451+, subdivisions (6)-(7) or (3) under each country
Occidental and oriental women. Christian and pagan
1161 General works
1164 Germanic
1166 Latin
1168 Slavic
1170 Muslim
1171 Oriental
1172 Jewish
Study and teaching. Women's studies
1180 General works
1181 By region or country, A-Z
General works
1201 Early to 1800
1800-
Scientific. Psychology, etc.
Cf. HV6046, The female offender
1206 English
1208 French
1210 German
1212 Italian
1214 Spanish
1216 Other
Aesthetics. Beauty in women. Beauty contests
Cf. RA778, Hygiene for women
1219 General works
1220 By region or country, A-Z
Practical. Ethics, etc.
1221 English
1223 French
1225 German. Dutch. Scandinavian
1227 Other
1229 For young women and girls
1233 General special (Special aspects of the subject as a whole)
1236 Women and the state
Cf. JX4211, Nationality of women
1381 Women and economics
1386 Women (i.e. the woman question) in literature
Class here works on the social relations and problems as affected by literature. For anthologies, literary biography or criticism (women as authors, or heroines of literature), see PN, PQ-PT
1389 Women in art

Women. Feminism - Continued
Women in public services
1390 General works
1391 By region or country, A-Z
Cf. JK-JQ, Women and the civil service
Women and religion
1393 General works
1394 Women and Christianity
1395 Women and the Bible
1397 Women in science and the arts
1399 Women and civilization
Cf. JX1965, Women and peace movements
Women in social reform, see HN49.W6
Women in industry, see HD6050+
By region or country
United States
1402 Periodicals. Societies. Serials
1403 Congresses
1406 Yearbooks
History
1410 General
Biography of reformers, etc.
1412 Collective
1413 Individual, A-Z
1416 Colonial period
1418 1776-1870
1419 1871-1920
1420 1920-
Reform literature, "Emancipation," etc.
1423 Early to 1860/70
1426 1860/70-
1438 By state, A-W
1439 By city, A-Z
1451-1870.5 Other regions or countries. Table IX 1/
Under each country:

10 nos.	5 nos.	1 no.	
(1)	(1)	.A1-5	Collections
(3)	(2)	.A6-Z7	History
(5)			Including general and modern history. For ancient, medieval, and renaissance history, see HQ1127+
			Biography of reformers, etc.
			.A3 Collective
	(3)		Reform literature, "Emancipation," etc.
(6)			Early through 1870
(7)			1871-
(9)	(4)	.Z8	By state, A-Z
(10)	(5)		By city, A-Z

1/ For Table IX, see pp. 135-144. Add country number in table to 1450

Women. Feminism

By region or country

1451-1870.5 Other regions or countries. Table IX 1/

Under each country: - Continued

2 nos.	
(1)	General
(2)	Local, A-Z

1870.8 Communist countries

.9 Underdeveloped areas

Women's clubs

Including women's organizations in general

For etiquette of women's clubs, see BJ2187

1871 Periodicals. Societies. Serials

1881 History

1883 Directories

1885 General works

Parliamentary law for women's clubs, see JF515

1901-2030:7 By region or country. Table V 1/

Under each country:

4 nos.	1 no.	
(1)	.A1A-Z	Periodicals. Societies. Serials For state federations (U.S.), see HQ1905
(2)	.A6-Z5	General works. History
(3)	.Z7	By state, A-Z
(4)	.Z9	By city, A-Z

1/ For Table IX, see pp. 135-144. Add country number in table to 1450

Including societies devoted primarily to the promotion of social intercourse and interests. For societies identified with special subjects in other classes, see the subjects

Societies
Class here general works only on societies of all kinds; when in doubt, see AS
1 Periodicals. Serials
5 Congresses
8 Yearbooks
10 Collected works (nonserial)
12 Dictionaries. Encyclopedias
17 Directories
25 History
35 General works, treatises, and advanced textbooks
Organization of societies, see AS6; for special subjects, see B-Z
By region or country
Under each country:
.A1-4 General works
.A5-Z Local, A-Z
61 United States
63 Canada and other British America
65 Other American countries, A-Z
67 Great Britain
71 Other European countries, A-Z
81 Asia, A-Z
84 Africa, A-Z
87 Australia and New Zealand
89 Pacific islands, A-Z
Secret societies
Periodicals. Serials
101 American and English
103 French
104 German
105 Italian
106 Other
110 Congresses
113 Yearbooks. Almanacs. Calendars
Collected works (nonserial)
115 Several authors
116 Individual authors
119 Dictionaries. Encyclopedias
Directories
121 General
By region or country
United States
122 General works
.3 By state, A-W
.5 By city, A-Z
123 Other regions or countries, A-Z
Under each country:
.x General works
.x2 By city, A-Z

Secret societies - Continued
History and description
125 General works
126 Other
128 Biography (Collective)
Secret societies of primitive races, see GN490.8
Ancient to A.D. 500
Cf. HS409, Freemasonry
131 General works
Mysteries, see BL610
Egyptian, see BL2450.M9
Eleusinian, see BL795.E5
137 Medieval to 1600
Knights of Malta, see CR4715+
Teutonic order, see CR4759+
Knights Templars, see HS741+
Rosicrucians, see BF1623.R7
142 Illuminati
Cf. HS259, Germany
Modern
145 General works
146 18th century
147 19th century
148 20th century

150 General works, treatises, and advanced textbooks
152 Fiction and miscellanea
153 Music
Cf. M1900+, Masonic
Rituals
Cf. HS455+, Freemasonry, etc.
155 Cipher rituals
157 Collections of rituals
Including "exposures"
158 "Side degrees." Burlesque rituals
Regalia
Cf. HS463+, Freemasonry, etc.
159 General works
160 Catalogs
161 Drill manuals
162 Halls and buildings
Cf. HS469, Freemasonry, etc.
164 Secret societies and the chruch
Cf. HS495, Freemasonry and the church
167 Secret societies and the state
Cf. HS481+, Freemasonry and the state
Anti-secret-society literature
For antimasonic, see HS473+, or HS525+
Periodicals. Serials
181 American and English
183 Other
Conventions
186 American
188 Other
191 Controversial literature

Secret societies - Continued

201-330.7 By region or country. Table V 1/

Under each country:

4 nos.	1 no.	
(1)	.A1-5	Collections
(2)	.A6-Z5	General works
(3)	.Z6A-Z	Special societies
(4)	.Z7A-Z	Local

Freemasons

Including masonry in general and "blue lodge" masonry in particular

Periodicals. Serials

351 American

353 English

355 French

357 German

359 Other

363 Societies, etc. (International)

365 Yearbooks

Cf. HS381+, Directories

Collected works (nonserial)

371 Several authors

373 Individual authors

375 Dictionaries. Encyclopedias

Directories and lists

381 General

By region or country

United States

383 General

385 By state, A-W

Under each:

.x General works

.x2 Counties, etc.

387 By city, A-Z

390 Other regions or countries, A-Z

Under each country:

.x General works

.x2 Local, A-Z

Study and teaching. Research

392 General works

393 Research lodges

Class here general works only; for special lodges, see the place

394 Musuems and collections

395 General works, treatises and advanced textbooks

396 Lodge organization and management

397 Addresses, essays, lectures

For collections of addresses, etc., see HS371+

Biography

Cf. HS509+, United States

HS557+, Other regions or countries

399 Collective

400 Individual, A-Z

For United States, see HS511

For Burns, see PR4300+

For Cagliostro, see BF1598.C2

1/ For Table V, see pp. 135-144. Add country number in table to 200

Freemasons - Continued
History and description
403 General works
405 Other
By period
407 Freemasonry among primitive races
Cf. GN490.8, Anthropology
409 Ancient, through A.D. 500
Cf. HS131, Secret societies
412 Medieval through 1600
Modern, 1601-
414 General works
18th century
416 General works
417 Special topics, A-Z
.A3 Adonhiramite masonry
418 19th and 20th centuries
420 Military and naval lodges
425 Symbolism and philosophy
427 Travels
431 Poetry. Drama
For Burns, see PR4300+
433 Art
435 Fiction. Humor. Satire

Masonic law
Including "Ancient constitutions"
For Ahiman Rezon, when general, containing only the Ancient constitution, see HS440; when published by a Grand lodge with such additions as to render it practically a state constitution, see HS445, under state, taking the number .A2
440 General works
442 Special topics, A-Z
By region or country, A-Z
United States
443 General works
445 By state, A-W
For by-laws of individual lodges, see HS539
.A2 Constitutions. By date
447 Other regions or countries, A-Z
451 Records and record blanks
Music, see M1900+
Rituals
Cf. HS155, Cipher rituals
455 "Monitors," etc., authorized. By state
457 Handbooks, instructors, "charts" (nonofficial)
459 Other
Including "exposures"
For Morgan's work, see HS525+

Freemasons - Continued
Regalia
Cf. HS159+, Secret societies
463 General works
465 Catalogs
467 Etiquette
469 Halls and buildings
Class here general works only; for special buildings, see local history
Cf. HS162, Secret societies
471 Masonic charities
Class here general works only. For local, see the country
Antimasonic literature
Cf. HS181+, Anti-secret-society literature
HS525+, Antimasonic controversy, 1827-1845
473 Periodicals. Societies. Serials
475 Other works
Freemasonry and the state
Cf. HS167, Secret societies and the state
481 General works
483 Law and legislation
485 By region or country, A-Z
Under each country:
.x General works
.x2 Law and legislation
491 Freemasonry and ancient mysteries
Cf. BL610, Mysteries
495 Freemasonry and the church
Cf. HS164, Secret societies and the church
499 Other special
e. g. Freemasonry and international law

By region or country
United States
503 Periodicals. Societies. Serials
505 Conventions
Biography
509 Collective
511 Individual, A-Z
History and description
515 General works
517 General special
By period
521 Colonial through 1759
523 1760-1827
Antimasonic controversy, 1827-1845
525 Histories
527 Controversial literature
529 1845-

Freemasons
By region or country
United States - Continued

537 By state, A-W
Under each:
.x Grand lodge publications, .A15-5
Proceedings
.A18 Early
Including compendiums and reprints
.A2 Serial
.A4 Reports. By date
.A42-49 Serial reports
.A5 Other. By date
.x2 General works. History
.x3 Other

539 By city, A-Z
For Washington, D.C., see HS537.D5
Under each:
.x General works
.x2 By lodge
Under each lodge:
(1) General works. History
(2) By-laws, etc. By date
(3) Other. By date

557-680.7 Other regions or countries. Table V 1/
Under each country:

4 nos.	1 no.	
(1).A2-4	.A1-4	Grand lodge proceedings
.A5-Z	.A5A-Z	History
(2)	.A6A-Z	Other general
(3)	.A7A-Z	By province, etc.
(4)	.A8-Z	By city

701-883 Other Masonic bodies and rites
Under HS701-780:
(1) Periodicals. Societies. Serials
(2) Collected works (nonserial)
(3) Directories
(5) History and collective biography
(7) Symbolism and philosophy
(9) Law
(10) Rituals
Including exposures
(12) Regalia
Including catalogs

1/ For Table V, see pp. 135-144. Add country number in table to 550

Freemasons

701-833 Other Masonic bodies and rites

Under HS701-780: - Continued

United States

(14) General

.A1-5 Publications of general grand chapter, council, etc.

Proceedings

.A18 Early

Including compendiums and reprints

.A2 Serial

.A3 Constitutions, etc. By date

.A4 Reports. By date

.A42-49 Serial reports, etc.

.A5 Other. By date

Under HS774, Scottish rite, use for publications of Supreme councils:

.A2, .A3, .A35, .A4 for Southern jurisdiction

.A5, .A6, .A65, .A7 for Northern jurisdiction

(17) By state, A-W

Including Treat Grant chapter, etc., publications like General chapter, etc.

(18) By city, A-Z

Under each:

.x General

.x2 Separate chapters, etc.

Under each:

(1) History

(2) By-laws, etc. By date

(3) Other. By date

(19) Other regions or countries, A-Z

Under each country:

.x General works

.x2 By city, A-Z

Divided like by chapter, etc., as in (18)

York rite

701-720 Chapter (Royal Arch Masons)

Including works on Chapter and Council

713 Order of high priesthood

721-740 Council (Cryptic masonry)

741-760 Knights Templars

751 Drill manuals

761-780 Scottish rite

For uncataloged Scottish rite material, see HS780.Z9

766 Cerneau organizations

825 Rites of Memphis and Mizraim

828 Martinist order

831 Rite of Swedenborg

833 Other rites, A-Z

Freemasons - Continued
Societies admitting Masons only. "Side degrees"
For Masonic clubs, see HS2725, etc.
835 Mystic shrine
.1 Periodicals. Societies. Serials
.3 History
.4 Law and legislation
.5 Rituals, etc.
By region or country
United States
.6 General works
.A2 Proceedings
.7 By state, A-W
.A2 Proceedings
.8 By city, A-Z
Under each:
.x General works
.x2 By temple, A-Z
.9 Other regions or countries, A-Z
Under each country:
.x General works
.x2 Local, A-Z
839 Red Cross of Constantine
Subarranged like HS835
841 Royal Order of Scotland
Subarranged like HS835
845 Other, A-Z
For the college fraternity Acacia, see LJ165.A4+
Adoptive masonry. Women in masonry
851 General works
853 Eastern Star
.1 Periodicals. Societies. Serials
.3 General works. History
.4 Law and legislation
.5 Rituals
By region or country
United States
.6 General works
.A2 Proceedings
.7 By state, A-W
.A2 Proceedings
.8 By city, A-Z
.9 Other regions or country, A-Z
Under each country:
.x General works
.x2 Local, A-Z
859 Other, A-Z
.A6 Order of the Amaranth
.D4 Order of Demolay for boys
Freemasonry among Blacks
875 Periodicals. Societies. Serials
877 Directories
878 General works. History
880 Law and legislation
882 Rituals

Freemasons
Freemasonry among Blacks - Continued
By region or country
United States
883 General works
887 By state, A-W
889 By city, A-Z
891 Other regions or countries, A-Z
Societies admitting masons only
893.A2 General works
.A3-Z Special, A-Z
Adoptive masonry
895.A2 General works
.A3-Z Societies
e. g. Eastern Star
Nonrecognized, "clandestine" masonry
901 Periodicals. Societies. Serials
906 Directories
911 General works. History
915 Law and legislation
917 Rituals
By region or country
United States
921 General works
925 By state, A-W
927 By city, A-Z
929 Other regions or countries, A-Z
Odd Fellows
Including General and Independent order in particular
951 Periodicals. Societies. Serials
953 Yearbooks
955 Collected works (nonserial)
959 Dictionaries. Encyclopedias
Directories
963 General
United States
967 General
969 By state, A-W
971 By city, A-Z
975 Other regions or countries, A-Z
981 General works, treatises, and advanced textbooks
983 Addresses, essays, lectures
History
987 General works
991 Biography
993 Symbolism and philosophy
995 Poetry
997 Fiction
1015 Music
Rituals
Cf. HS155+, Secret societies
Authorized
1019.A2 Book of forms
.A4 Other general
.A6 Special ceremonies
1021 Other
Including "exposures"

Odd Fellows - Continued
Regalia
Cf. HS159+, Secret societies
1025 General works
1026 Catalogs
1029 Buildings and halls
Cf. HS162, Secret societies
1030 Charitable institutions
Class here general works only; for local, **see** country
1031 Works against Odd Fellowship
Cf. HS1021, Exposures
By region or country
United States
1041 General
.A2 Proceedings of Sovereign Grand Lodge
.A3-5 Other publications
Cf. HS714+, United States
1043 By state, A-W
.A2 Proceedings of Grand Lodges
.A3-5 Other publications
1045 By city, A-Z
Under each:
.x General
.x2 By lodge
Under each:
(1) History
(2) By-laws, etc. By date
(3) Other. By date
1051 Other regions or countries, A-Z
Under each country:
.x General works
.x2 By place, A-Z
Related bodies
Under each order in HS1061+:

(1) Periodicals. Societies. Serials
(2) Directories
(3) General works. History
(4) Law
(5) Rituals
By region or country
United States
(6) General works
(7) By state, A-W
(8) By city, A-Z
(9) Other regions or countries, A-Z
Under each country:
.x Geneal works
.x2 Local, A-Z

For the English orders substitute:
England
(6) General
(7) By city, A-Z

1061-1070 Patriarchal Odd Fellowship (Encampment)
1071-1080 Patriarchs Militant
1101-1110 Manchester Unity (England)
1111-1120 Grand United Order (England)

Odd Fellows
Related bodies - Continued
1131+ Other English bodies (one number each)
Subdivided:
.A2 Proceedings
.A4 Constitutions, by-laws, etc.
.A5 Rituals
.A7 Other general
.A8-Z Local
Under each place:
.A2-5 General works
.A6-Z By lodge
Societies admitting Odd Fellows only. "Side degrees"
1151 Improved Order of Muscovites
Subarranged like HS835
1159 Other, A-Z
.07 Oriental Order of Humility and Perfection
Adoptive bodies
1161 Daughters of Rebekah
Subarranged like HS835
1169 Other adoptive bodies, A-Z
e. g. .L3 Ladies Auxiliary, Patriarchs Militant Independent Order of Odd Fellows
Oddfellowship among Blacks
1171 Grand United Order (United States)
Subdivided like HS835
1175 Household of Ruth
Subdivided like HS835
1179 Other, A-Z
Knights of Pythias
1201 Periodicals. Societies. Serials
1203 Collected works (nonserial)
1205 Dictionaries. Encyclopedias
Directories
1207 General works
By region or country
United States
1208 General works
1209 By state, A-W
1210 By city, A-Z
1213 Other regions or countries, A-Z
Under each country:
.x General works
.x2 Local, A-Z
1216 General works, treatises, and advanced textbooks
1217 Addresses, essays, lectures
1219 History
1220 Symbolism and philosophy
Rituals
Cf. HS155, Cipher rituals
1231 Authorized
1233 Other
Including "exposures"
Regalia
Cf. HS159+, Secret societies (General)
1235 General works
1236 Catalogs

Knights of Pythias - Continued

1238 Buildings and halls

1241 Charitable institutions

Class here general works only; for local, see the country in HS1254 and HS1261

By region or country

United States

1251 General works

1253 By state, A-W

.A2-5 Proceedings of Grand lodges

1254 By place, A-Z

Under each:

.x General works

.x2 Separate lodges, A-Z

1261 Other regions or countries, A-Z

Under each country:

.x General works

.x2 Local, A-Z

Affiliated bodies

1271-1280 Endowment rank

1281-1290 Uniform rank

Under each:

(1) Periodicals. Societies. Serials

(2) Directories

(3) General works. History

(4) Law and legislation

(5) Rituals

By region or country

United States

(6) General works

(7) By state, A-W

(8) By city, A-Z

(9) Other regions or countries, A-Z

1350 Other, A-Z

Under each:

(1) Periodicals. Societies. Serials

(2) Rituals

(3) History and description

1355 Other societies, A-Z

Under each (using successive Cutter numbers):

.x Periodicals. Societies. Serials

.x2 Rituals

.x3 History and description

.x4 By region or country, A-Z

e. g. .S6-64 Sociedad Abakua

Other societes. By classes

Benevolent and "friendly" societies and mututual assessment fraternities

Cf. HD7090+, Workingmen's insurance, social insurance, etc.

1501 Periodicals. Serials

Class here general only; for organs of particular societies, see the societies

1502 Congresses

1503 Directories, yearbooks, etc.

1505 Law and legislation. By region or country, A-Z

Other societies. By classes
Benevolent and "friendly" societies and mutual assessment fraternities - Continued
History and description
1506 General works
By region or country
United States
1507.A1-3 General works
.A5-W By state, A-W
1508 Other regions or countries, A-Z
1510 By society, A-Z
Under each:
I. Larger societies
(1) Proceedings and periodicals
(2) Laws and constitutions
.A1-5 General
.A6-Z By minor jurisdiction, generally state
Subarranged by date
(3) Rituals and regalia
(4) General works. History
Including local
(5) Other. By date
II. Smaller societies
(1) Proceedings and periodicals
(2) Rituals. By date
(3) General works. History
Note 1. Under (1) in both I and II the general scheme of arrangement is to be:
.A1-19 Periodicals. Societies. Serials
.A2-49 Proceedings of "grand" lodge
[.A5 Laws and constitutions, in II only]
.A7-W Proceedings. By date
.Z6-8 Directories
Proceedings of a ladies' auxiliary are placed with the main order
Note 2. In assigning numbers, use for the more important societies one figure as a basis, e. g. Red men, .R3, .R32, .R33, etc.; for smaller societies two figures, e. g. Knights of golden rule, .G68, .G682, .G683
Note 3. Example
Improved order of red men, .R3-35
.R3A2 Proceedings of Great council in United States
.R3A25 Proceedings of Great council, U.S. Pocahontas degree
.R3N7 Proceedings of Great Council, New York
.R3N75 Proceedings of Great Council, New York, Pocahontas degree
.R3N752 Reports to Great council, New York, Pocahontas degree
.R32A3 General laws, 1845
1845
.R32O3 Laws for Ohio
.R33R Red men, illustrated (Ritual)
.R34L History, by L-

Other societies. By classes

Benevolent and "friendly" societies and mutual assessment fraternities

1510 By society, A-Z

II. Smaller societies - Continued

Note 4. Arrange "Foresters" and allied societies as follows:

.F72-726 Ancient order of Foresters, A.O.F.

.F73-736 Canadian order of Foresters, 1879-

.F74-746 Ancient order of Foresters of America, F.O.A. 1889-

Including Knights of Sherwood Forest, Ancient order of shepherds, Companions of the forest, Junior foresters of America

.F76-766 Independent order of Foresters, 1874-

Including Miriam degree, Glenwood degree, Juvenile branch, Royal foresters

.F79-793 United order of Foresters, 1881-1884

.F794-796 United order of Foresters, 1894-

Religious societies

Including societies formed by members of a particular church, e. g. Knights of Columbus

For church auxiliary societies, see BV, BX

1525 Collected works (nonserial)

1527 Directories

1529 General works. History

By church

Under each:

(1) General

.A2-29 Periodicals. Societies. Serials

.A3-5 Directories

.A6-Z Other

(2) General societies, A-Z

Including American and foreign 1/

By region or country

United States

(3) General societies, A-Z 1/

In United States only

(4) Local societies. By place, A-Z 1/

(5) Other regions or countries, A-Z

Under each country:

.x General societies, A-Z 1/

.x2 Local societies. By place, A-Z 1/

1536-1540 Catholic

1546-1550 Protestant

For individual denominations, see BX

1556-1560 Mohammedan. Mussulman

1/ Subarranged liked HS1510

Other societies. By classes - Continued

Race societies

Including societies formed by persons of a particular nationality living in a foreign country, except when membership is restricted to a religious community. For historical societies, see D-F

1601 Collected works (nonserial)
1605 Directories
1610 General works. History

By nationality

Under each:

(1) General
- .A2-29 Periodicals. Societies. Serials
- .A3-5 Directories
- .A6-Z Other

(2) General societies, A-Z 1/
Including American and foreign

By region or country

United States

(3) General societies, A-Z 1/
In United States only

(4) Local societies. By place, A-Z 1/

(5) Other regions or countries, A-Z
Under each country (using successive Cutter numbers):
- .x General societies, A-Z 1/
- .x2 Local societies at capital, A-Z 1/
- .x3 Other local societies. By place, A-Z 1/

1701-1705 American
1711-1715 Canadian
1721-1725 Spanish-American
1801-1805 English
1806-1810 Scotch
1811-1815 Irish
1816-1820 Welsh
Western and Southern Europe (Romanic nations)
1836-1840 Belgian (except Flemish)
1841-1845 French
1846-1850 Italian
1856-1860 Spanish and Portuguese
Northern and Central Europe (Germanic nations)
1876-1880 Swiss
1886-1890 Austrian
1891-1895 Dutch and Flemish
1896-1900 German
1911-1915 Scandinavian
1916-1920 Danish
1921-1925 Norwegian
1926-1930 Swedish
1951-1955 Finnish
1966-1970 Hungarian

1/ Subarranged like HS1510

Other societies. By classes
Race societies
By nationality - Continued
Eastern Europe (Slavic nations)
1996-2000 Bohemian
2006-2010 Lithuanian
2016-2020 Polish
2026-2030 Russian
2036-2040 Serbian
2041-2045 Bulgarian
2046 Other, A-Z
e. g. .L3 Latvian
.S5 Slovenian
Southeastern Europe
2051-2055 Albania
2061-2065 Greek
2071-2075 Romanian
Western and Southwestern Asia
2096-2100 Turkish
2116-2120 Armenian
2136-2140 Syrian
Eastern Asia
2176-2180 Chinese
2186-2190 Japanese
2196-2200 Philippine
By race
2226-2230 Jewish
Subarranged like HS1701-1705
Black
Cf. HS875+, Freemasonry among Blacks
HS1171+, Oddfellowship among Blacks
2253 Periodicals. Societies. Serials
2255 Directories
2257 General works. History
By region or country
United States
2259 General societies, A-Z 1/
2261 Local societies. By place, A-Z 1/
2265 Other regions or countries, A-Z
Under each country:
.x General societies, A-Z 1/
.x2 Local societies. By place, A-Z 1/
Occupation societies (not elsewhere provided for)
In case of doubt, see HD or S
Farmers' societies, see HD and S
Trade unions and employers' associations, see HD
2275 General works
Political and "patriotic" societies
2301 Collected works (nonserial)
2303 Directories
2310 General works. History
2312 International societies, A-Z

1/ Subarranged like HS1510

Other societies. By classes

Political and "patriotic" societies - Continued

By region or country

United States

2321 Periodicals. Societies. Serials

2322 Congresses

2323 Dictionaries. Yearbooks, etc.

2324 Law and legislation

2325 General works. History

2328 By state, A-W

.A1-3 Regions

2329 By city, A-Z

2330 By society, A-Z 1/

e. g. .K6-63 Knights of the Ku Klux Klan

2337-2460.7 Other regions or countries. Table V 2/

Under each country:

4 nos.	1 no.	
(1)	.A1-29	Collected works (nonserial)
(2)	.A4	General works. History
(3)	.A5-Z6	Societies, A-Z 1/
(4)	.Z9	Local, A-Z

Clubs

2501 Periodicals. Societies. Serials

2503 Yearbooks, etc.

Directories

2507 General

By region or country

United States

2509 General

2511 By state, A-W

2513 By city, A-Z

2515 Other regions or countries, A-Z

Under each country:

.x General

.x2 By city, A-Z

2519 General works. History and description

2521 Theory. Psychology, etc.

Particular types

Including books about clubs. For club publications, see HS2721+

Army and navy, see U, V

Athletic clubs, see GV

2567 Commercial clubs

2581 Country clubs

Literary clubs, see P

Political clubs, see J and HS2301+

Press clubs, see PN

Scientific clubs, see Q-QR

Women's clubs, see HQ1871+

International clubs

2701 General works

2705 By club, A-Z

1/ Subarranged like HS1510

2/ For Table V, see pp. 135-144. Add country number in table to 2330

Clubs - Continued
By region or country
Under each country:
Periodicals, see HS2501
(1) Yearbooks, etc.
Directories, see HS2507+
(3) General works. History
(4) By state, A-W
(5) By city, A-Z
Arrange clubs alphabetically under city, reserving .A1-5 for general works; under each club use:
(1) Annuals and other serials
(2) General works. History
(3) Other. By date

2721-2725	United States
2731-2735	Canada
2735.5	Latin America
2736-2740	Mexico
2741-2745	West Indies
2756-2760	Central America
2776-2780	South America
2851-2855	Europe
2861-2865	Great Britain
2886-2890	Austria. Austro-Hungarian Empire
2901-2905	France
2911-2915	Germany
2941-2945	Greece
2946-2950	Italy
2956-2960	Netherlands (Belgium and Holland)
2971-2975	Russia
2981-2985	Scandinavia
2986-2990	Denmark
2991-2995	Norway
2996-3000	Sweden
3000.2-.6	Iceland
3001-3005	Spain and Portugal
3011-3015	Switzerland
3016-3020	Bulgaria
3021-3025	Romania
3026-3030	Yugoslavia
3031-3035	Turkey
3040	Other European regions or countries, A-Z
3051-3055	Asia
3061-3065	India
3071-3075	China
3076-3080	Japan
3081-3085	Korea
3091-3095	Russia in Asia
3115	Other Asian regions or countries, A-Z
3125-3130	Africa
3131-3135	British possessions
3141-3145	French possessions
3151-3155	German possessions (Former)
3165	Other African regions or countries, A-Z
3171-3175	Australia and New Zealand
3196-3200	Pacific islands

Clubs and societies for special classes
Class here when not with special class
Boys' societies
Cf. HV878, Boys' clubs
For boys' societies affiliated with fraternal orders see HS859, HS1169, etc.
Not reformatory in purpose
3301 Periodicals. Societies. Serials
3308 General works. History and description
Special societies
Boy scouts
For works about Boy Scouts in war, see D639.B6, D810.B7, DS921.5.B6, etc.
3312 General works
Boy Scouts of America
3313.A1-19 Proceedings, annual reports, etc.
.A3 Constitutions, bylaws of BSA. By date
.A4A-Z Periodicals. By title
.A5 Jamborees, congresses. By date
.A6-Z5 General works
.Z6A-Z Leaders and committees
.Z7A-Z Ranks, offices
.Z8A-Z Uniforms, insignia
.Z9A-Z Awards, etc.
Including Order of the Arrows and religious awards
.Z95A-Z Merit badges
Cub Scouts 1/
3314 General works
.5 Webelas 1/
3315 Explorers 1/
Cf. VK544, Sea scouting
3316 Other regions or countries, A-Z
Other societies
By region or country
United States
3319 General works
3320 By state, A-W
3321 By city, A-Z
3325 Other regions or countries, A-Z
Under each country:
.x General works
.x2 By society, A-Z
Girls' societies
Cf. HV879, Girls' clubs
3341 Periodicals. Societies. Serials
3345 Directories
3348 General works. History and description
3353 General societies
For girls' societies affiliated with fraternal orders see HS859, HS1169, etc.

1/ Subarranged like HS3313.A6-Z95

Clubs and societies for special classes
Girls' societies - Continued
By region or country
United States
3359 General works
3360 By state, A-W
3361 By city, A-Z
3365 Other regions or countries, A-Z
Women's societies, see HQ1871+

COMMUNITIES

51 Periodicals. Serials
53 Societies
55 Congresses
57 Collected works (nonserial)
(63) Study and teaching. Schools, etc., see H62+, HM45+, HT109, HT411, HV11
65 General works
By region or country, see HN

URBAN GROUPS. THE CITY. URBAN SOCIOLOGY

Class here works dealing generally with the city as a social group. For special aspects of the city, see HT or elsewhere as indicated below
Cf. GT3420+, Town life (Manners and customs)
For individual cities, see D-DU, HC, HN, J, JS, etc.
For urban geography, see GF125
For urban anthropology, see GN505

101 Periodicals. Serials
103 Yearbooks
105 Societies
107 Congresses
108 Collected works (nonserial
.5 Dictionaries. Encyclopedias
109 Study and teaching. Schools, exhibitions, museums
110 Research
History
111 General
113 General special
By period
114 The ancient city
Cf. CB311, Ancient civilization
JC51+, Ancient state (Political theory)
JS58, Local government
For individual cities, see D-F
115 Medieval cities
Cf. CB351+, Medieval civilization
JC101+, The Medieval state
JS61, Local government
119 Modern cities
By region or country
Including documents
America
121 General works
North America
122 General works
123 United States
.5 By region or state, A-Z
By city, see HN80
127 Canada

Urban groups. The city. Urban sociology
History
By region or country
America - Continued
Latin America
127.5 General works
.7 Mexico
Central America
128.A2A-Z General works
.A3-Z By region or country, A-Z
.5 West Indies. Caribbean area
.A2A-Z General works
.A3-Z By country or island, A-Z
South America
129.A2A-Z General works
.A3-Z By region or country, A-Z
Europe
131 General works
133 Great Britain
135 France
137 Germany
145 Other, A-Z
147 Asia, A-Z
.5 Arab countries (Collectively)
Africa
148.A2A-Z General works
.A3-Z By region or country, A-Z
149 Australia and Pacific islands, A-Z
150 The international city (Projects)
151 General works. "The city problem"
153 General special
155 Addresses, essays, lectures
Garden cities. "The city beautiful"
Including residence cities and suburbs, e. g. Letchworth; most of the general works are classified here. For model industrial villages, see HD7526+
161 General works
164 By region or country, A-Z
165 By city, A-Z
City planning
Class here works dealing predominantly with the social, economic, and political factors involved in city planning. For works emphasizing architectural and engineering aspects, see NA9000+ and TD160+
Cf. HE305+, Urban transportation
HT170+, Urban renewal. Urban redevelopment
Study and teaching. Research
165.5 General works
By region or country
.52 United States
.53 Other regions or countries, A-Z
166 General works

Urban groups. The city. Urban sociology
City planning - Continued
By region or country
United States
167 General works
.2 Department of Housing and Urban Development
.5 By region or state, A-Z
168 By city, A-Z
169 Other regions or countries, A-Z
Under each country:
.x General works
.x2 Local, A-Z
.5 Underdeveloped areas
Zoning
Cf. HD1393.6, Real estate business
.6 General works
By region or country
United States
.7 General works
.72 By region or state, A-Z
.73 By city, A-Z
.8 Other regions or countries, A-Z
Under each country:
.x General works
.x2 Local, A-Z
.9 Special topics, A-Z
.D4 Development rights transfer
Housing, see HD7285+, NA7511+
Slums, see HV4023+
Settlements, see HV4175+
Public works, see HD4421+, TD21+
Public buildings, see JS201+, NA4201+, NA4430+
Streets, see HE369+
Parks, see SB481+
Transportation and community development, see HE148
Municipal industries, see HD4421+
Municipal art, see NA9000+
Urban renewal. Urban redevelopment
170 General works
By region or country
United States
175 General works
176 By region or state, A-Z
177 By city, A-Z
178 Other regions or countries, A-Z
Under each country:
.x General works
.x2 Local, A-Z
City population
For statistics, see HB2161+
201 General works
Children in cities
206 General works
Education, see LC5101+
Playgrounds, see GV421+
Cf. HT281, Recreation, amusements
Juvenile delinquency, see HV9051+

Urban groups. The city. Urban sociology
City population - Continued
215 Immigration
221 Race question in cities
City charities, see HV1+
Police, see HV7988+
City hygiene, see RA566.7
231 Effect of city life
Liquor problem, see HV5001+
Markets, see HF5470+
Removal of waste, see TD571+
Sewerage, see RA585+; TD514
Water supply, see RA591+, TD201+
Mental and moral life
251 General works
255 City and culture
City and education, see LC5101+
265 City morals
Cf. HQ101+, Prostitution
HV6177, Cities and crime
City and religion, "The city church," see BV637+
281 Recreation. Amusements
Cf. HT206, Children in cities
Political significance
Municipal government, see JS
Municipal corruption, see JS231; HV6310
Municipal finance, see HJ9000+
Civic reform, see JS
The city as an economic factor
321 General works
325 City promotion
Cf. HF6161.M8, Advertising by municipalities
The city as a social factor, see HT151
By region or country, see HT122+
Cf. HN51+, Social history
Metropolitan areas
330 General works
334 By region or country, A-Z
351 Suburban cities and towns
City and country
For statistical studies, see HB1951+
361 General works
371 Growth of cities
381 Movement to the country
384 By region or country, A-Z
Regional planning
Cf. GF90+, Landscape assessment
390 Periodicals. Societies. Serials
391 General works

Urban groups. The city. Urban sociology
Regional planning - Continued
By region or country
United States
392 General works
.5 By interstate region, A-Z
For interstate metropolitan areas, see HT394
.A7 Appalachian region
.A8 Atlantic States
.C42 Lake Champlain region
.C45 Chesapeake Bay region
.G7 Great Lakes Region
.G74 Great Plains
.M54 Minnesota-Wisconsin
.M6 Mo-Kan
.N4 New England
.P3 Pacific Northwest
.P4 Penjerdel
.P6 Potomac Valley
.S65 Southern States
.T3 Lake Tahoe region
.T46 Tennessee Valley
.T7 Tri-State region (New York, New Jersey, Conneticut)
393 By state, A-W
Under each:
.x General
.x2 Local, A-Z
394 By metropolitan area, A-Z
395 Other regions or countries, A-Z
Under each country:
.x General works
.x2 By region, province, state, etc., A-Z
.x3 By metropolitan area, A-Z

RURAL GROUPS. RURAL SOCIOLOGY

Cf. GF127, Rural geography
GT3470, Country life (Manners and customs)

401 Periodicals. Serials
403 Yearbooks
405 Societies
407 Congresses
409 Collected works (nonserial)
411 Study and teaching. Schools, exhibitions, museums
415 History
421 General works. "Country life"
Including the sociological aspect; for light literature, see S521
423 Addresses, essays, lectures
Social betterment in the country, see HT421+
The country village and country town
Cf. JS271+, Local government
431 General works
Village communities, see JC31+

Rural groups. Rural sociology - Continued
Rural housing, see HD7289, NA7600+
Country roads, see HE355.3, TE229+
Rural free delivery, see HE6455+
Country population
For statistics, see HB2371+
451 General works
453 Children in the country
455 Immigration
Rural police, see HV7965+
Rural hygiene, see RA427+, RA771
Mental and moral life
461 General works
Country schools, see LB1566+, LB1621, LB2861, LC5146+
465 Country morals
Country and village churches, see BV638+
469 Recreation. Amusements
471 The rural district in politics
475 The rural district as an economic factor
The rural district as a social factor, see HT421
485 Social centers in the country

CLASSES

601 Periodicals. Serials
603 Societies
605 Collected works (nonserial)
607 History
608 Research
609 General works
611 Addresses, essays, lectures
By region or country, see HN43+
Origin of social classes
621 General works
Birth, see HT641+
Occupation, see HT675+
627 Geographical conditions
631 Historical conditions
635 Property. Economic basis
Cf. HB831, Leisure classes
Classes arising from birth
Cf. CR3499+, Titles of honor, rank, precedence, etc.
641 General works
645 Royalty
Cf. JC385, Theory of kingship
Nobility. Aristocracy
Cf. JC411+, Political theory
647 General works
650 Military class
653 By region or country, A-Z
Commons
655 General works
657 Gentry
Middle class, see HT680+
Working class, see HD4841+
Serfs, see HT751+
Slaves, see HT851+

Classes - Continued
Classes arising from occupation
675 General works
Middle class
680 Periodicals. Societies. Serials
681 Collected works (nonserial)
682 Congresses
684 General works
Agricultural, see HD1506+
Commercial, see HF
685 Industrial
687 Professional
Cf. B, K, L, R, etc., for special professions
690 By region or country, A-Z
Including documents
Working class proletariate, see HD4841+, HD4901+
Outcasts, "classes maudites," see GT6550+
Caste system
713 General works
720 India
Cf. DS422.C3, History
725 Other regions or countries, A-Z
731 Freedmen
Serfdom
751 General works
753 Addresses, essays, lectures
757 Origin of serfdom
761 Extinction of serfdom
By period
Ancient, see HT863
775 Medieval and modern
By region or country
781 Great Britain
785 France
Germany
791 General works
795 Prussia
801 Other states, A-Z
803 Austria. Austro-Hungarian Empire
Russia
807 General works
Emancipation, 1861, see DK222
815 Other regions or countries, A-Z
Contract labor, peonage, see HD4871+

Slavery
Including slavery and serfdom
Class works on Black slavery with general works on slavery, HT871+
851 Periodicals. Serials
853 Societies
855 Congresses
857 Collected works (nonserial)
History
861 General
863 Ancient
865 Middle Ages
867 Modern

Classes
Slavery - Continued
869 Biography of slaves
Ct. HT1029, Biography of abolitionists
General works
871 English
873 French
875 German
877 Italian
879 Spanish and Portuguese
881 Dutch and Scandinavian
883 Other languages, A-Z
891 Addresses, essays, lectures
893 Poetry, etc.
Economic aspects of slavery
For slave labor, see HD4861+
901 General works
905 Plantation management
Social aspects of slavery, see HT871+

Religion and slavery
910 General works
Christianity and slavery
913 General works
915 Bible and slavery
917 Individual sects, A-Z
919 Islam and slavery
921 Other religions
Race and slavery
925 General works
Black slavery, see HT871+
929 Other races
Law of slavery
941 General works
943 International law
Cf. JX4447, Maritime law
945 General special
950 By region or country, A-Z
The slave trade
Periodicals, see HT851
Societies, see HT853
Congresses, see HT855
Collections, see HT857
General works. History
975 General
979 Ancient
983 Middle Ages
Modern
985 General works
African, see HT1322
991 Addresses, essays, lectures
Suppression of slave trade
Cf. JX4447, Maritime law
For works on the abolition of the slave trade by any country, see the country, e. g. HT1162, Great Britain
993 General works
999 Cases

Classes
Slavery - Continued
Abolition of slavery. Anti-slavery
Periodicals, see HT851
Societies, see HT853
Congresses, see HT855
Collected works (nonserial), see HT857

1025	History
	Biography of abolitionists
1029.A3	Collective
.A4-Z	Individual, A-Z
1031	General works
1033	Addresses, essays, lectures
	Influence of economic conditions, see HT901
	Influence of religion, see HT910+
1037	Conditions under emancipation
	By region or country, see HT1048

By region or country
Under each country:

5 nos.	3 nos.	2 nos.	1 no.	
(1).A1-6	(1)	(1).A1-6	.A1-6	Documents
.A7-Z		.A7-Z	.A7-Z8	History and general works
(2)	(2)			Slave trade and its suppression
(3)	(3)			Abolition of slavery and conditions under emancipation
(4)		(2).A-Z4	.Z9A-Z	Local, A-Z
(5)		.Z5A-Z		Colonies

1048-1050	America
	Including "Asiento" contract
	Use also for North America and Spanish America
	United States, see E
1051-1052	Canada
1052.5	Latin America
1053-1054	Mexico
1055-1056	Central America
1071-1073	West Indies
1076-1080	Cuba
	Including works treating Cuba and Puerto Rico together
1081-1085	Santo Domingo. Dominican Republic
1086-1090	Puerto Rico
1091-1093	British West Indies
	Cf. HT1165, British colonies
1096-1100	Jamaica
1105	Other, A-Z
1107-1108	French West Indies
1112-1113	Dutch West Indies
1119	Other islands, A-Z
	South America
1121	General works
1122-1123	Argentina
1124-1125	Bolivia
1126-1130	Brazil
1131-1132	Chile

Classes
Slavery
By region or country 1/
South America - Continued
1133-1134 Colombia
1135-1136 Ecuador
1137 Guiana
1139-1140 British
1141-1142 Dutch
1143-1144 French
1145-1146 Paraguay
1147-1148 Peru
1149-1150 Uruguay
1151-1152 Venezuela
Europe
1155 General works
1161-1165 Great Britain
For works on the British colonies, see HT1165
For works on individual colonies, see the special geographical divisions
1171-1175 Austria. Austro-Hungarian Empire
1176-1180 France
1181-1185 Germany
1191-1195 Italy
Netherlands (Low Countries)
1196-1200 Belgium
1201-1205 Netherlands (Holland)
1206-1210 Russia
1211-1215 Scandinavia
1216-1220 Spain
1221-1225 Portugal
1227-1228 Switzerland
Balkan States
1231 General works
1232 Bulgaria
1234 Greece
1235 Montenegro
1236 Romania
1237 Serbia
1238-1239 Turkey
1240 Other European countries, A-Z
Asia
1241-1245 China
1245.5 Taiwan
Former British possessions
1246-1249 India
1250 Other, A-Z
1261-1265 Indochina
1266-1270 Indonesia
1271-1275 Philippines
1276-1280 Japan
1286-1290 Iran
1291-1295 Soviet Union in Asia
1296-1300 Central Asia
1301-1305 Siberia
1306-1310 Turkey in Asia
1315 Other divisions of Asia, A-Z
1317 Arab countries

1/ For subarrangement, see p. 52

Classes
Slavery
By region or country 1/ - Continued
1321-1323 Africa
1326-1330 East Coast
1331-1335 West Coast. Guinea Coast
1336-1337 Abyssinia. Ethiopia
1341-1343 Barbary States
1345 Slavery of white captives. Personal narratives, etc.
Cf. G530, Shipwrecks
1346-1350 Morocco
1351-1355 Algeria
1356-1360 Tunis
1361-1365 Tripoli
1366-1370 Zaire
Cf. DT639, Congo River
1371-1375 Egypt
1376-1380 Liberia
1381-1385 Sahara and Sudan
1391-1395 British possessions
1396-1400 French possessions
1401-1405 German possessions (Former)
1406-1410 Italian possessions
1416-1420 Portuguese possessions
1421-1425 Spanish possessions
1427 Other divisions of Africa, A-Z
1431-1435 Australia
1441-1445 Pacific islands

RACES

Including the race as a social group and race relations in general

1501 Periodicals. Serials
1503 Societies
.A3 General
1505 Congresses
1506 Study and teaching
1507 History
1521 General works. Race conflicts. Race prejudice
1523 General special
Special phases
Meaning and origin of race, marks of race, race and color, see GN
Economics of race questions
1531 General works
Races and labor, see HD8081, etc.
Races and immigration, see JV6208, JV6348, etc.
Races and intoxicants, see HV5198+

1/ For subarrangement, see p. 52

Races
Special phases - Continued
Race societies, see HS1601+
Protection of native races, see HV3176+
Race questions in international law, see JX
Race questions and colonization, see JV261+, JV305+, JV533+, etc.
1561 Ethics of race questions

By race
Caucasic
Scientific works, see GN537
1575 General works
1577 Aryan. Indo-European
Cf. GN539, Anthropology
Black. Hamitic
1581.A2 Periodicals. Societies. Serials
.A3-Z General works
Ethnological works
Scientific works, see GN
1589 Popular works. Scriptural ethnology
By region or country, see E185.61, United States; D-DU, Other regions or countries
Semitic, Jewish, see GN547, DS101+
Mongolian, see GN548, DS
1595 Other, A-Z
Cf. GN549, Anthropology
By region or country
United States, see E185.8, F, HD8080, etc.
Other regions or countries, see D-DU, HC, HD

Periodicals. Serials
1 English
2 French
3 German
4 Other
Yearbooks, see HV35
Cf. H9, Social sciences (General)
6 Societies (International). Associations (International)
7 Directories (International
8 Congresses (International)
10 Exhibitions. Museums
.5 Social work as a profession
11 Study and teaching. Schools
.5 Examinations, questions, etc.
12 Dictionaries. Encyclopedias
Collected works (nonserial)
13 Several authors
15 Individual authors
History of philanthropy
Including public welfare
Cf. HG4028.C6, Corporate contributions to charity
16 General
17 Jewish philanthropy
Ancient
19 General
20 By region or country, A-Z
22 Medieval through 1800
25 1801-
Biography
27 Collective
Including general and United States
Cf. HV98+, United States (Local)
HV101+, Other regions or countries, subdivision (7) or (3) under each country
28 Individual, A-Z
29 Statistics: Theory and method
Cf. HV85+, United States
Treatises
30 Early through 1870
31 1871-
33 Dependent, defective, and delinquent classes. Abnormal man
Cf. HV4961+, Degeneration
35 Handbooks, manuals, etc.
37 Addresses, essays, lectures
For collected essays, see HV13+
38 Plays, pageants, etc.
Charity organization and practice
40 General works
41 General special
e. g. Fund raising
43 Social case work. Friendly visiting
45 Social group work

Charity organization and practice - Continued
48 Private relief
Public relief
Cf. HV70+, State regulation of charities
51 General works
53 Regulations
55 Poor-law guardians
57 Elberfeld system
Institutional care. Indoor relief
59 General works
61 Poorhouses
Cf. HV8748+, Workhouses
65 Noninstitutional care. Outdoor relief
Class here general works only; for special, see HV85+
Rural social work
67 General works
By region or country, see HV85+
Work relief
Cf. HD1516, Agricultural colonization
HD3840+, Public works
HV8748+, Workhouses
69 General works
By region or country, see HV85+
State regulation of charities. Public welfare laws
Cf. HV51+, Social pathology
70 General works
71 International relations
72 State grants and subventions

By region or country
For poor in large cities, slums, etc., see HV4023+
United States
Documents. Collections
Including documents relating specifically to charities
85 General
86 State
Including counties
87 City
88 Societies. Associations
Including state "conferences"
Cf. HV99, subdivision (2)

By region or country
United States - Continued
89 Yearbooks, directories, etc.
90 Statistics
Class monographs and studies here; for serial collections of tables, etc., see HV85+
91 General works. History
Biography, see HV27+, HV98+
95 Policy, etc.
National institutions
97.A3A-Z General works
.A4-Z By institution, foundation, etc., A-Z
e. g. .C6 Commonwealth Fund
98 By state, A-W
Including reports of individual state institutions and collective biography
Cf. HV86, State documents other than reports of institutions
HV88, State conferences
99 By city, A-Z
Including collective biography
For documents, see HV87
State and city in HV98 and HV99 are subdivided:
.x General works
.x2 Particular institutions
Including associated charities, charity organization societies, etc.
Note:
For documents relating to American charities in general, see HV85
For documents relating to all charities in a given state, or to several of them, see HV86. Reports of Boards of charities, etc., should be placed here, even if at the time the board has only one institution under its supervision
For documents relating to all charities in a given city, or to several of them, see HV87. Reports of city Boards of charities, etc., should be treated like state boards
For reports of separate institutions, even if documentary in form, see the institution in HV98 or HV99
For nonofficial works on American charities in general, see HV90, HV91, HV95, according to subject matter
For nonofficial works on the charities of a state, see HV98, under the state, subdivision (1); under subdivision (2) put reports of public institutions, supported by the state and ministering to the whole or part of the state
For nonofficial works on the charities of a place, see HV99, under the place, subdivision (1)

By region or country
United States
99 By city, A-Z
Note: - Continued
For reports of, and works on, particular private charities, see HV99 under place, subdivision (2), even if state-wide in scope
Special rule for the District of Columbia:
Put documents, serial (except reports) and non-serial in HV86
Put general nonofficial material, and nonofficial works relating to a particular institution in HV99, Washington (1) or (2)
Put reports of separate institutions in HV99, Washington (2) even if documentary in form
101-520.5 Other regions or countries. Table IX 1/
Under each country:

10 nos.	5 nos.	1 no.	
			Documents
(1)	(1)	.A1-5	General
(2)			State, see (9) or (4)
(3)			City, see (1) or (5)
(4)	(2)		Societies. Associations. Congresses. Conferences For local, see subdivision (10) or (5)
(5)	(3)	.A6-Z7	General works. History. Statistics Other than serial collections of tables which are in subdivisions (1), (9)-(10), or (1), (4)-(5)
	.A2		Yearbooks, directories, handbooks, etc.
(7)			Biography (Collective) For local, see HV101+, subdivisions (9), (10) or (4), (5) Individual biography, see HV28
(8)			Policy, etc. See also (5)

1/ For Table IX, see pp. 135-144. Add country number in table to 100

By region or country
101-520.5 Other regions or countries. Table IX 1/
Under each country: - Continued

10 nos.	5 nos.	1 no.	
(9)	(4)	.Z8	By state, A-W Under each (using successive Cutter numbers): Documents .x Serial .x2 Special .x3 Societies. Associations .x4 General works. History, policy, etc.
(10)	(5)	.Z9	By city, A-Z

530 The church and charity
541 Women and charity
544 Charity fairs
Cf. HF5470+, Markets. Fairs
Social settlements, see HV4175+
Salvation Army, see HV4330+
.5 International social works
Cf. HC60+, Technical assistance
HV553+, Disaster and refugee relief
For individual countries or regions receiving relief, see HV85+
547 Self-help groups
Relief in case of disasters
553 General works
554 Evacuation of civilians
.4 Church and disaster relief
555 By region or country, A-Z
For United States use:
.U6 General
.U62 Local, A-Z
Red Cross. Red Crescent
Cf. JX1381, Brussels Conference, 1875
JX5136, Treatment of wounded. Geneva and Hague conventions
For war activities of the Red Cross, including its origin, see UH535+
Official reports
560 Serial
563 Special. By date
568 General works. History
Biography
569.A1A-Z Collective
.Z2-Z Individual, A-Z
e. g. .B3 Barton, Clara
571 Other

1/ For Table IX, see pp. 135-144. Add country number in table to 100

Relief in case of disasters
Red Cross. Red Crescent - Continued
By region or country
Under each country:
Official reports
(1) Serial
(2) Special. By date
(3) General works. History
(4) Other
575-578 United States
579 By region, state, city, A-Z
580 Other regions or countries, A-Z
583 Junior Red Cross
Other associations
589 International
590 United States
593 Other regions or countries, A-Z
Special types of disasters
Including organization of relief, reports of committees, etc.
For description, narratives, etc., see D-F, HC
For societies, etc., see HV555+
600 Earthquakes. By date
Subarranged by place
610 Floods. By date
.A3 Plans for relief
620 Fires. By date
Epidemics, see RA649+
Famines
For special cases, see HC
630 General works
635 Distribution of seed, grain, etc.
636 Storms, hurricanes, typhoons, etc. By date
638 Mine disasters
639 War
For war relief in a particular war, see the war
For war refugees (General), see HV640+; for a particular war, see the war
Refugee problems
Refugee relief
Including relief for persons who have fled for refuge or safety to a foreign country in time of war or for reasons of race, religion, nationality, or political convictions
640 General works
.3 International Refugee Organization
.4 By country providing relief, A-Z
For relief given to only one ethnic or national group, see HV640.5
.5 By ethnic or national group receiving relief, A-Z
e. g. .A6 Arab refugees
645 Church and refugee problems

Life saving
Cf. VK1300+, Life saving service at sea
650 Official documents
656 Associations, International
For local, see HV670
660 General works. History
664 Other
670 By region or country, A-Z
Under each country:
.x Associations
Under each:
(a) Serial reports
(b) Special. By date
(c) General works. History
(d) Other
.x2 General works. History
.A1-17 Documents
.x3 Other

Prevention of accidents
675 General works
.5 Juvenile works
By region or country
United States
675.A1 Periodicals. Societies. Serials
.A2 General works
.A3 By state, A-W
.A4-Z By city
677 Other regions or countries, A-Z
Under each country:
.x General works
.x2 Local, A-Z
First aid to the injured, see RC86+

Free professional services
Legal aid
680 General works
By region or country
United States
682.A1-19 Periodicals. Societies. Serials
.A5A-Z Monographs
.A6-Z By city
Under each:
.x General works
.x2 Particular institutions, A-Z
685 Other regions or countries, A-Z
Medical charities
Social service to the sick
Cf. HV3000+, Protection, assistance and relief of incurables
687.A2 Periodicals. Societies. Serials
.A3-Z General works
.5 By region or country, A-Z

Free professional services
Medical charities - Continued
Medical advice and aid
Cf. HD710+, Public medical care plans
HV1450+, Services to the aged
RA413.7.A4, Private medical care plans

688.A2 General works
.A3-Z By region or country, A-Z
Under each country:
.x General works
.x2 By city, A-Z

689 Psychiatric social work

691 Free nursing
Subarranged like HV688

Free dispensaries, see RA960+

694 Diet kitchens
Subarranged like HV688

696 Other, A-Z
.C5 Clothing relief
.D6 Drinking fountains
.F4 Flower guilds
.F6 Food relief
Cf. TX946, Mass feeding
.F85 Fresh air funds
Cf. HV931+, Children
.R2 Reading for the sick
.R4 Repatriation
.S4 Seashore and country homes
.S5 Shut-in societies
.S6 Soup kitchens
.T55 Transients' relief
.T7 Traveler's aids

PROTECTION, ASSISTANCE AND RELIEF

Special classes. By age
Families. Mothers. Widow's pensions

697 General works
By region or country
699 United States
700 Other regions or countries, A-Z
.5 Unmarried mothers
.7 Unmarried fathers

Children
Cf. HQ767.8+, The family
LC4001+, Handicapped children

701 Periodicals. Serials
703 Societies. Associations
Collections
705 Documents
706 Monographs, etc.
707 Congresses (International)
709 Exhibitions

Protection, assistance and relief
Special classes. By age
Children - Continued

711 Dictionaries. Encyclopedias
713 General works
715 General special (Special aspects of the subject as a whole)

741-803 By region or country
Under each country (except United States):

2nos.	1 no.	
(1).A1-19	.A1-5	Periodicals. Serials
.A2-29		Societies. Associations For local societies and associations, see the locality
		Documents
.A3-39		Serials
.A4		Monographs. By date
.A5-59		Collected works (nonserial)
.A6A-Z	.A6-Z7	General works. History, etc.
.A7-Z	.Z8	By state, province, etc., A-Z
(2)	.Z9	By city, A-Z

United States
741 General works
742 By region or state, A-Z
Class here boards of child and animal protection; e. g. Colorado, Montana, West Virginia, Wyoming
For table of regions, see p. 147
For table of states, see p. 148
743 By city, A-Z
Under each:
.x General works
.x2 Institutions, A-Z
745-746 Canada
747 Other American regions or countries, A-Z
Europe
749 General works
751-752 Great Britain
755-756 Scotland
757-758 Ireland
759-760 Austria. Austro-Hungarian Empire
761-762 France
Germany
763 General works
764 By city, A-Z
765 Baden
766 Bavaria
767 Prussia
769 Saxony
770 Wurttemberg
771 Other, A-Z
772-773 Greece
774-775 Italy

Protection, assistance and relief
  Special classes. By age
    Children
      By region or country 1/
        Europe - Continued
776-777 Netherlands. Low Countries
778-779 Netherlands. Holland
780-781 Belgium
782-783 Soviet Union
784-785 Scandinavia
786-787 Denmark
788-789 Norway
790-791 Sweden
792-793 Spain
794-795 Portugal
796-797 Switzerland
799 Other European regions or countries, A-Z
800 Asia. By region or country, A-Z
801 Africa. By region or country, A-Z
802 Australia
.5 New Zealand
803 Pacific islands, A-Z

Lying-in-hospitals, see RG12+
Foundlings
835 General works
  By region or country
    United States
838 General works
841 By region or state, A-Z
844 By city, A-Z
    Other regions or countries
      Under each country:
        .x General works
        .x2 Local, A-Z
Day nurseries. Foster day care
  Cf. LB1140, Nursery schools
851 General works
  By region or country
    United States
854 General works
857 By region or state, A-Z
859 By city, A-Z
    Other regions or countries
      Under each country:
        .x General works
        .x2 Local, A-Z
867 Baby farming
868 Milk depots
  Cf. HD4501.M5, Municipal industry
    LB3473+, Feeding of school children
Children's playground, see GV421+
Chimney-sweeps, see HV873+
Blind, deaf and dumb, see HV1551+

1/ For subarrangement, see p. 64

Protection, assistance and relief
Special classes. By age
Children - Continued
Destitute, neglected, and abandoned children.
Aid and homes
873 General works
875 Adoption and care in private families, etc.
876 Junior Republics
Boys
877 General works
878 Boys' clubs, etc.
Cf. HQ796+, Children's rights
HS3340+, Boys' societies
879 Girls
Cf. HQ796+, Children's rights
HS3341+, Girls' societies
Special institutions, see HV885+
By region or country
United States
880 Periodicals. Societies. Serials
881 General works
883 By region or state, A-Z
885 By city, A-Z
887 Other regions or countries, A-Z
Under each country:
.x General works
.x2 Local, A-Z
Education of children, see LC4501+

Handicapped children
888 General works
By region or country
United States
.5 General works
889 By region or state, A-Z
.5 By city, A-Z
890 Other regions or countries, A-Z
Under each country:
.x General works
.x2 Local, A-Z
Mentally handicapped children. Developmentally disabled children
891 General works
By region or country
United States
894 General works
897 By region or state, A-Z
899 By city, A-Z
901 Other regions or countries, A-Z
Under each country:
.x General works
.x2 Local, A-Z

Protection, assistance and relief
Special classes. By age
Children
Handicapped children - Continued
Physically handicapped children
Cf. RD701+, Orthopedic surgery
903 General works
By region or country
United States
904 General works
905 By region or state, A-Z
906 By city, A-Z
907 Other regions or countries, A-Z
Under each country:
.x General works
.x2 Local, A-Z
Fresh-air funds
Including "Country weeks," etc.
931 General works
By region or country
United States
934 General works
936 By region or state, A-Z
938 By city, A-Z
Under each:
.x General works
.x2 Special. By name of resort, A-Z
941 Other regions or countries, A-Z
Under each country:
.x General works
.x2 Local, A-Z
Hospitals and asylums, see RD705
Migrant workers' children, see HV873+
Newsboys, see HV873+
Orphanages. Orphans
Including general works on institutional care
959 Collected works (nonserial)
961 General works. History
963 Early through 1800
965 1801-
By region or country
United States
971 Collected works (nonserial)
975 Societies (General). Associations (General)
General works. History
978 General
981 Early through 1800
983 1801-
986 Other
990 By region or state, A-Z
995 By city and county, A-Z
Under each:
.x General works
.x2 Particular institutions, A-Z

Protection, assistance and relief
Special classes. By age
Children
Orphanages. Orphans - Continued

1001-1420.5 Other regions or countries. Table IX 1/

10 nos.	5 nos.	2 nos.	1 no.	
(1)	(1)		.A1-5	Collected works (nonserial)
(4)	(2)	(1)	.A6-Z7	General works Including history
(5)				Early through 1800
(6)				1801-
(8)	(3)			Other
		(2)		Local, A-Z
(9)	(4)		.Z8	By region or state, A-Z
(10)	(5)			By city, A-Z Under each state or city: .x General works .x2 Particular institutions, A-Z

Sick children. Free dispensaries, etc., see RJ27+

Young men and women
For Y.M.C.A. and Y.W.C.A., see BV1000+

1421 General works
1423 Young men
1425 Young women
By region or country
United States
1431 General works
1435 By region or state, A-Z
1437 By city, A-Z
1441 Other regions or countries, A-Z
Under each country:
.x General works
.x2 Local, A-Z

Women

1442 Periodicals. Societies. Serials
.5 Congresses
1443 Directories
1444 General works
By region or country
United States
1445 General works
1446 By region or state, A-Z
1447 By city, A-Z

1/ For Table IX, see pp. 135-144. Add country number of table to 1000

Protection, assistance and relief
Special classes. By age
Women
By region or country - Continued
1448 Other regions or countries, A-Z
Under each country:
.x General works
.x2 Local, A-Z
Aged
Including medical advice and aid
Cf. GT3100, Manners and customs
For blind aged, see HV1597.5
For contributory old age pensions, see HD7105+
For private medical care plans, see RA413.7.A4
For private old age insurance, see HG9426+
For public medical care plans, see HD7101+
1450 Directories
1451 General works
1453 History (General)
By region or country
United States
General works
1457 Periodicals. Societies. Serials
1461 General works
1465 Other
1468 By region or state, A-Z
1471 By city, A-Z
Under each:
(1) General works
(2) Particular institutions, A-Z
Other regions or countries
Under each country:
(1) Periodicals. Societies. Serials
(2) General works. History
(3) Other
(4) By region or state, A-Z
(5) By city, A-Z
Canada
1475.A1-3 Dominion
.A4-Z Provinces
1478 Other American regions or countries, A-Z
1481 Europe. By region or country, A-Z
1484 Asia. By region or country, A-Z
1487 Africa. By region or country, A-Z
1490 Australia, A-Z
1493 Pacific islands, A-Z
Handicapped
Including general works on the blind, deaf, mentally handicapped and physically handicapped
Cf.HV888+, Handicapped children
RC435+, Mentally ill
1551 Periodicals. Societies. Serials
1552 History

Protection, assistance and relief
Handicapped - Continued
By region or country
United States
1553 General works
1555 By region or state, A-Z
1559 Other regions or countries, A-Z
1568 General works
Marriage of the handicapped, see HQ1036+
Blind
Including works on the deaf and blind
1571 Periodicals. Serials
Class here works other than those of local institutions
Cf. HV1783, United States
1573 Societies (International). Associations (International)
1575 Congresses (International)
1576 Museums. Exhibitions. By date
1577 Collected works (nonserial)
1578 Dictionaries. Encyclopedias
1581 History

Biography
Including personal experiences, achievements, etc.
For biography of educators and pq9yhs, see HV1623+; for special regions or countries, see HV1792 and HV1801+, subdivision (7) or (3) under each region or country
1584 Collective
Individual, see HV1792; HV1801+, subdivision (7) or (3) under each country
General works
1591 Early through 1800
1593 1801-
Essays
1595 Early works through 1800
1596 1801-
1597 Deaf-blind
For biography of educators and pupils, see HV1623+
.5 Aged (Blind and visually handicapped)
1598 General special (Special aspects of the subject as a whole)
Marriage of the blind, see HQ1038
1601 The state and the blind
Cf. HV85+, State boards of charities, etc.
For documents, see HV1785+; HV1801+, subdivisions (1) - (3) or (1) under each country

Protection, assistance and relief
Handicapped
Blind - Continued
Education of the blind
Periodicals, serials, see HV1571
Documents, see note, HV1601
1618 History and statistics
Biography of educators, philanthropists, etc., and exceptional pupils
Cf. HV1792, United States, etc.
1623 Collective
1624 Individual, A-Z
e. g. .K4 Keller, Helen
1626 General works
Practice
1631 General works
Methods
1638 General works
1643 Elementary, kindergartens, etc.
1646 Secondary
1649 Advanced
Professional and industrial
Including vocational guidance
1652 General works
1655 Professions
1658 Industries
1661 Home education
Systems of typography, writing, etc.
Printing houses
1667.A1-29 General works
.A3-Z Individual
Under each:
.x Reports
.x2 Other
1668 Choice of type. Uniformity. Controversial works
Forms of type
Braille
1669 General works
1672 American Braille
1674 Other special, A-Z
e. g. .07 Oriental Braille
1675 New York Point
1678 Moon
1681 Boston Line
1684 Mascaró
1687 Ideographic
Lists of books, see Z5346
1691 Stenographic systems
Music, see MT38
1698 Other
1701 Apparatus, writing machines, punctographs, etc.
1708 Other
e. g. Comparative study of braille and talking book reading

Protection, assistance and relief
Handicapped
Blind - Continued
Books for the blind. Talking books
Class here public policy including government support programs
For libraries for the blind:
Administration and description, see Z675.B8; for history, statistics, reports, see Z731+
For catalogs and bibliographies of books and talking books, see Z5346+
For Library of Congress collection of books for the blind, see HV2250+
1721 General works
By region or country
1731 United States
1735 Canada
1739 Other American regions or countries, A-Z
1743 Europe. By region or country, A-Z
1747 Asia. By region or country, A-Z
1751 Africa. By region or country, A-Z
1756 Australia, A-Z
Recreation for the blind
1765 General works
1766 Recreation for children
1767 Physical education, games, etc.
1768 Concerts
1771 Readings
1774 Lectures
1779 Other
e. g. Use of museums
1780 Other topics, A-Z
.S4 Seeing eye dogs
By region or country
Class here schools and asylums
United States
1783 Periodicals.
For school periodicals, see HV1796
Documents
Class here national documents only; for state documents, see HV1796
1785 Serials
1786 Special
1788 Societies. Associations
Including state and municipal associations
1789 Congresses
1790 Directories
1791 History. Statistics
Biography
Cf. HV1623+, Biography of educators, philanthropists, etc. and exceptional pupils
1792.A3 Collective
.A4-Z Individual, A-Z
1793 Policy
1795 General works

Protection, assistance and relief
Handicapped
Blind
By region or country
United States - Continued

1796 By region or state, A-Z
Under each state:
(1) General works
Including state documents
(2) State institutions
(3) Other institutions. By place
e. g. New York
.N7A-Z General works
.N71-75 State asylums
.N760-799 Other institutions. Alphabetically by place

1801-2220.5 Other regions or countries. Table IX 1/
Under each country:

10 nos.	5 nos.	2 nos.	1 no.	
				Periodicals. Serials
(1)	(1)		.A1-A5	General
(2)				State
(3)				City
(4)	(2)			Societies. Associations. Conferences For local, see (10)
(5)	(3)	(1)	.A6-Z7	General works Including history
(7)				Biography, A-Z Cf. HV1623+, Biography of educators, etc. .A3 Collective
(8)				Policy, etc.
		(2)		Local, A-Z
(9)	(4)		.Z8	By region or state, A-Z
(10)	(5)			By city, A-Z Under each city: (1) General works (2) Individual societies and institutions Class here all individual institutions

1/ For Table IX, see pp. 135-144. Add country number in table to 1800

Protection, assistance and relief
Handicapped
Blind
(2250-2329) Library of Congress collection of books for the blind
By type, in same order as HV1696+
Subarranged under each:
(0) Periodicals and other general and miscellaneous (A)
(1) Religion and philosophy (B)
(2) History and biography (C - F)
(3) Geography and travels (G)
(4) Social sciences (H - L)
(5) Art. Graphic arts (N)
(6) Music (M)
(7) Literature (P)
(8) Science (Q)
(9) Useful arts (R - V)
For example:
HV2250-2259 Braille
2250 Periodicals. Societies. Serials
2251 Religion and philosophy
2252 History and biography
2253 Geography and travels
2254 Social sciences
2255 Art
2256 Music
2257 Literature
2258 Science
2259 Useful arts
2260-2269 American Braille, etc.
2349 Pamphlets not cataloged
Deaf
Including deaf-mutes
For deaf and blind, see HV1571+
2350 Periodicals. Serials
2353 Collected works (nonserial)
Societies (International). Associations (International)
2354 General works
2356 Volta Bureau
2359 Congresses (International)
2362 Exhibitions
2365 Dictionaries. Encyclopedias
History
2368 Early through 1800
2370 1801-
Biography
For biography of educators, see HV2423+
For special regions or countries, see HV2534 and HV2571+, subdivision (7) or (3) under each country
2373 Collective
Individual, see HV 2534, and HV2571+, subdivision (7) or (3) under each country

Protection, assistance and relief
Handicapped
Deaf - Continued
General works
2377 Early through 1800
2380 1801-
2390 Addresses, essays, lectures
2395 General special (Special aspects of the subject as a whole)
Deaf and psychiatry, see RC451.4.D4
Marriage of the deaf, see HQ1040
2401 The state and the deaf
Education of the deaf
Class here general works and theory only; for schools, see HV2561 and HV2571+, subdivision (10) or (5), under each country
Periodicals, serials, see HV2350; HV2510
Documents, see HV2353; HV2515+
Societies, see HV2354; HV2522+
2417 History
Cf. HV2368, Early history
Biography of educators, philanthropists, etc.
2423 Collective
2426 Individual, A-Z
2430 General works

Practice
2437 General works
Methods
2440 General works
2443 Elementary, kindergarten
2446 Secondary
2449 Advanced
Professional and industrial
2452 General works
2455 Professions
2458 Industries
2461 Public school classes
2463 Other special methods. By author
2465 Home education
2468 Elementary textbooks
2469 Special subjects, A-Z
.A7 Arithmetic
.A73 Art
.B45 Bengali language
.D36 Danish language
.E5 English language

.G4 German language
.J3 Japanese language
.R4 Reading

.S94 Swedish language

Protection, assistance and relief
Handicapped
Deaf
Education of the deaf - Continued
Systems of speech, etc.
2471 General works
Special
Sign language
2474 General works
2475 Dictionaries. Encyclopedias
2476 Juvenile works
Manual speech
2477 General works
2480 Alphabets
Oral systems
2483 General works
2487 Lip reading
2490 Visible speech
2493 Aural method for semi-deaf
2497 Combined system
2500 Other
Institutions, schools, see HV2561; HV2571+, subdivisions (10) or (5) under each country
Apparatus, ear-trumpets, audiphones, etc., see RF300+
2508 Theater for the deaf. Sigh language theater

By region or country
United States
2510 Periodicals. Serials
For school periodicals, see HV2561
Documents
Cf. HV2350, Periodicals
2515 Periodicals. Serials
2518 Special
State documents, see HV 2561
2522 Societies. Associations
2526 Congresses. Conferences
2530 History. Statistics
Biography
2534.A3 Collective
.A4-Z Individual, A-Z
2537 Policy
General works
2541 Early through 1800
2545 1801-
2551 Other
2561 By region or state, A-Z
Under each state:
(1) General works
(2) State institutions
(3) Other institutions. By city, A-Z

Protection, assistance and relief
Handicapped
Deaf
By region or country - Continued

2571-2990.5 Other regions or countries. Table IX 1/
Under each country:

10 nos.	5 nos.	2 nos.	1 no.	
				Periodicals. Serials
(1)	(1)	(1)	.A1-5	General
(2)				State
(3)				City
(4)	(2)			Societies. Associations
(5)				Congresses. Conferences
(6)	(3)	(1)	.A6-Z7	General works. History. Statistics
(7)				Biography, A-Z .A3 Collective
(8)				Policy
		(2)		Local, A-Z
(9)	(4)		.Z8	By region or state, A-Z
(10)	(5)			By city, A-Z Under each city: (1) General works (2) Particular institutions

Incurables
3000 General works
By region or country
Under each country, subdivided like HV3006+
3001 United States
3003 Other regions or countries, A-Z

Mentally handicapped. Developmentally disabled
Cf. HV891+, Mentally handicapped children
RC570+, Mental deficiency
3004 General works
3005 Vocational training, occupations and employment for the mentally handicapped
Marriage of the mentally handicapped, see HQ1041
.5 Transportation
By region or country
United States
3006.A1 Documents
.A2 Periodicals. Serials
.A3 Societies, conferences, etc.
.A4 General works
.A56-W By region or state
Under each state:
(1) General works
(2) Institutions. By place, A-Z
3008 Other regions or countries, A-Z
Under each country:
(1) General works
(2) Institutions. By place, A-Z

1/ For Table IX, see pp. 135-144. Add country number in table to 2570

Protection, assistance and relief
Handicapped - Continued
Mentally handicapped. Developmentally disabled - Continued
3009 The mentally handicapped and poverty
General works on the mentally ill and psychiatric hospitals, see RC435+

Physically handicapped
Cf. HD7255+, Rehabilitation of disabled workmen
RD701+, Orthopedic surgery
UB360+, Provision for disabled soldiers
3011 General works
Personal narratives and biography, see CT9987, RD796
Physically handicapped children, see HV903+
Occupations for the physically handicapped
3018 General works
3019 By occupation, A-Z
3022 Transportation and travel
By region or country
United States
3023.A1A-Z Documents
.A2A-Z Periodicals, serials, societies, conferences, etc.
.A3A-Z General works
.A4-Z By region or state, A-Z
Under each state:
.x General works
.x2 Institutions. By place, A-Z
3024 Other regions or countries, A-Z
Each country subarranged like HV3023.A4-Z
Special classes. By occupation
Seamen
Cf. VB290+, Sailors' homes
3025 General works
3031-3163 By region or country. Table V, modified 1/
Under each country:

4 nos.	1 no.	
(1)	.A2-39	Periodicals. Societies. Serials
		Associations, snug harbors, etc.
(2)	.A4A-Z	General works
(3)	.A5A-Z	Local institutions. By place, A-Z
(4)	.A6-Z	Other

NOTE 1. For Pacific islands use HV3163.A-Z

Soldiers, see UB, UH
For rehabilitation of disabled soldiers and sailors, see UB360+

1/ For Table V, see pp. 135-144. Add country number in table to 3030

Protection, assistance and relief
Special classes. By occupation - Continued
Shop women, clerks, etc.
Cf. HD6053+, Women labor
3165 General works
3167 Holidays
3169 Rest hours
3170 Noon lunches, etc.
Institutions, etc.
3171 General works
3172 United States. By place, A-Z
3173 Other regions or countries, A-Z
3174 Other. By occupation, A-Z
Except as otherwise provided for in Classes B - Z
e. g. Teachers in LB
Under each:
.x General works
.x2 United States
.x3 Other
.A5 Actors
.F5 Fishermen
.F8 Furriers
Intellectuals, see .P7
.M48 Migrant laborers
.M5 Miners
.M6 Motion picture employees
.P7 Professionals, intellectuals, scholars
.R3 Railroad workers
Scholars, see .P7
.S8 Surveyors
Special classes. By race or ethnic group
Cf. HS1601+, Race societies
For specific types of charities, see HV1571+, HV2349
3176 General works
3177 Local. Associations and institutions. By place, A-Z
Special race or ethnic group
Indians, see E91+
Afro-Americans
3181 General works
3185 Local. Associations and institutions. By place, A-Z
Jews
3190 General works
By region or country
United States
3191 General works
3192 By place, A-Z
3193 Other regions or countries, A-Z
Irish (in United States)
3194.A2 General works
.A3-Z By place
3197 Scotch (in United States)
Subdivided like HV3194
3198 Other (in United States)
Subdivided like HV3194
3199 Other, A-Z
Under each:
.x General works
.x2 By region or country, A-Z

Protection, assistance and relief - Continued
Immigrants
Class here chiefly associations and institutions
Cf. JV6325+, Promotion and assistance to immigrants (General)
4005 General works
By region or country
United States
Cf. JV6526+, Promotion and assistance to immigrants (General)
4010 General works
4011 By region or state, A-Z
4012 By city, A-Z
4013 Other regions or countries, A-Z

Poor in cities. Slums
For tenements, the housing question, see HD7285+
4023 History
4028 General works
4030 Other
4041-4170.7 By region or country. Table V 1/
Under each country:

4 nos.	1 no.	
(1)	.A2A-Z	Periodicals. Societies. Serials
(2)	.A3A-Z	History
(3)	.A5A-Z	General works
(3.5)	.A6A-Z	By province, etc., A-Z
(4)	.A7-Z	By city

Social settlements. College settlements, etc.
4175 Periodicals. Societies. Serials
4178 Congresses. Conferences
4180 History
4183 General works
4187 Other
4189 Social work. Practice
4191-4320.7 By region or country. Table V 1/
Under each country:

4 nos.	1 no.	
(1)	.A2A-Z	Periodicals. Serials
(2)	.A3A-Z	History
(3)	.A4A-Z	General works
(3.5)	.A6A-Z	By province, etc., A-Z
(4)	.A7-Z	By city

1/ For Table V, see pp. 135-144. Add country number in table to 4040 or 4190, as the case requires

Protection, assistance and relief

Poor in cities. Slums - Continued

Salvation Army and the city poor

Cf. BX9701+, Salvation Army

4330 Periodicals. Societies. Serials

For mission journals, see BV

4331 History

Biography, see BX9741+

4337 General works

4341-4470.7 By region or country. Table V 1/

Under each country:

4 nos.	1 no.	
(1)	.A2A-Z	Periodicals. Serials
(2)	.A3A-Z	History
(3)	.A4A-Z	General works
(3.5)	.A6A-Z	By province, etc., A-Z
(4)	.A7-Z	By city

Agricultural colonization, see HD1516

Mendicancy. Vagabondism. Tramps

Including welfare work for homeless transients

For the poor (General), see HV1+

History

4480 General works

4483 Ancient

4485 Medieval

4488 Modern

General works

4491 Early through 1800

4493 1801-

4501-4630 By region or country. Table V 1/

Under each country:

4 nos.	1 no.	
(1)	.A1-29	Periodicals. Societies. Serials
(2)	.A3A-Z	History. Statistics
(3)	.A4	General works, etc.
(4)	.A5-Z	Local, A-Z

Pauperism and crime, see HV6174

Pauperism and lunacy, see HV3009

Protection of animals

For protection of children and animals, see HV742

4701 Periodicals. Serials

4702 Societies

4703 Collected works (nonserial)

4704 Congresses

4705 History, statistics, etc.

1/ For Table V, see pp. 135-144. Add country number in table to 4340 or 4500, as the care requires

Protection, assistance and relief
Protection of animals - Continued

	General works
4707	Early through 1800
4708	1801-
	Addresses, essays, lectures
4711.A1-Z8	General
.Z9	Uncataloged leaflets, pamphlets, etc.
4712	Study and teaching. Humane education
	Law and legislation, see K
	The Bible and animals, see BS663+
	Humane treatment of animals
4731	Merciful killing
4733	Transportation
4735	Advice regarding care of animals
	Classes
	Birds, see QL676.5, SK351+
4743	Cats
4746	Dogs
	Horses
4749	General works
4751	Injurious harness, bits, etc.
4753	Docking
4755	Other special
4758	Other
4761-4890.7	By region of country. Table V 1/

Under each country:

4 nos.	1 no.	
(1)	.A2A-Z	Societies. Associations
(2)	.A3A-Z	General works, history, etc.
(3)	.A5A-Z	By region or state Including state societies
(4)	.A6-Z	By city, A-Z Under each city: .x General works .x2 Particular institutions

	Anti-vivisection
	For vivisection as a scientific method, see QP45
4905	Periodicals. Serials Cf. HV4701, Protection of animals
4908	Societies Cf. HV4702, Protection of animals
4911	Documents
4913	Congresses Cf. HV4704, Protection of animals
4915	General works. History
	Miscellany
4918.A1-Z4	General works
.Z5	Uncataloged leaflets, pamphlets, etc.
	Law and legislation, see K

1/ For Table V, see pp. 135-144. Add country number in table to 4760

Protection, assistance and relief
Anti-vivisection - Continued
By region or country
United States
4925 Periodicals. Serials
4926 Societies
4928 Documents, Federal
4930 General works. History, etc.
4931 Controversial works
4932 Other
4933 States, A-W
Under each:
.x Societies
.x2 Documents
.x3 Monographs. By date

Other regions or countries
Under each country:
(1) Documents
(2) General works. History, etc.
(3) Controversial works, etc.
(4) By place, A-Z
4935 Canada
4939 Other American regions or countries, A-Z
4943 Europe. By region or country, A-Z
4947 Asia. By region or country, A-Z
4951 Africa. By region or country, A-Z
4955 Australia, A-Z
4959 Pacific islands, A-Z

DEGENERATION

Cf. HM111, Sociology
HV33, Dependent, defective and delinquent classes
HV891+, Mentally handicapped children
HV1551+, Handicapped
HV5050+, Social degeneration and alcoholism
HV6001+, Criminology
QH528, Biology

4961 Collected works (nonserial)
4962 History
Cf. HQ71+, Sexual deviations
4963 General works (Modern)
Treatises
Scientific
4965 General works
4967 Stigmata (General)
4969 Popular, etc.
Special
4973 Physical degeneration and stigmata
Mental degeneration and stigmata
4975 General works
4977 Degeneration and insanity
Degeneration and genius, see BF426
4979 Moral degeneration and stigmata
4981 Inbreeding. Consanguineous marriages
Cf. HQ1026+, The family
4983 Mixed marriages
Cf. HQ1031, The family
Marriage of degenerates and defectives, see HQ1036+
4987 Family degeneration. Atavism
Cf. HV6123+, Criminal anthropology
4989 Eugenic sterilization
4991 Child study. Child degeneration
Cf. HV9069+, Juvenile offenders
LB1101+, Educational psychology
LC4001+, Handicapped children
4993 Other
4995 By region or country, A-Z
Under each country:
Collections
.xA1-5 Periodicals. Serials
.xA6-7 Documents
.x2 General works
.x3 Special topics, A-Z
.x4 Local, A-Z

ALCOHOLISM. INTEMPERANCE. TEMPERANCE REFORM

For Prohibition Party, see JK2381+
For medical works, see RC565

5001 Periodicals. Serials
Class here scientific works only; for others (Propaganda, etc.), see HV5203, HV5285, and HV5301+, subdivision (1) under each country
5002 Yearbooks
5006 Societies (International)
5009 Congresses (International)
Collected works (nonserial)
5012 Documents (treating of several countries)
5015 Monographs. Papers of individual authors
5017 Encyclopedias and dictionaries
History
5020 General works
5022 Ancient
5023 Medieval through 1600
5025 19th-20th centuries
5028 Statistics
Biography of reformers
Cf. HV5215+, Women and temperance reform
HV5232, Alcoholism
HV5293, Intemperance
HV5301+, Alcoholism by region or country
5030 Collective
5032 Individual, A-Z
Activity not limited to one country
e. g. .M3 Mathew, Theobold
.M8 Murphy, T. E.
.S3 Smith, E. T.

General works, treatises, and advance textbooks
5033 Early through 1800
Scientific
5035 English
5036 French
5037 German
5038 Italian
5039 Scandinavian
5043 Other languages, A-Z
5045 Psychology of alcholism
5047 Addresses, essays, lectures
Social degeneration and alcoholism
5050 General works
Alcoholism and crime
5053 General works
5055 Responsibility of alcoholics
Alcoholism and disease. Alcoholism and insanity, see RC367+
Popular physiological
Including "Temperance teaching"
5060 English
5061 French
5062 German
5065 Other languages, A-Z

Alcoholism. Intemperance. Temperance reform - Continued
5066 Juvenile works
Miscellany. Stories, dialogues, etc.
5068 Narratives. Tales. Allegories
5069 Plays. Dialogues. Church services
5070 Poems
For songs with music or indication of tunes, see M2198+
5071 Recitations, etc.
5072 Other. Essays, lectures, sermons, etc.
Alcoholism and the state. Regulation, control
Law and legislation, see K
5081 General works
Practice. Methods of regulation and control
Cf. HX550.L7, Socialism and the liquor problem
5082 General works
Taxation. License. Local option
5084 General works
United States
5085 General works
5086 By region or state, A-Z
By city, see HV5298
5087 Other regions or countries, A-Z
Prohibition
Including controversial literature
5088 General works
United States
For periodicals, serials, see HV5285
5089 General works
5090 By region or state, A-Z
5091 Other regions or countries, A-Z
Gothenburg system
5092 General works
United States
5093 General works
5094 Local, A-Z
5095 Other regions or countries, A-Z
Alcoholism and economics
5101 General works
5103 Statistics
United States
5105 General works
5106 By region or state, A-Z
5107 By city, A-Z
5110 Other regions or countries, A-Z
Special topics
Alcoholism and the laboring classes
5115 General works
5118 By region or country, A-Z
5121 Other, A-Z
Alcoholism and education
5125 General works
5128 By region or country, A-Z
5132 Alcohol and the family
5133 Alcoholism and the child
5135 Alcohol and youth
5137 Alcohol and women
5138 Alcohol and the aged

Alcoholism. Intemperance. Temperance reform - Continued
5141 Alcoholism and genius
Cf. HV5045, Psychology of alcoholism
Alcoholism and the army
5145 General works
By region or country
5148 United States
For discussion of the army canteen, see UC753
5151 General works
5157 Special topics, A-Z
5162 Other regions or countries, A-Z
Alcoholism and the navy
5165 General works
By region or country
United States
5167 General works
5168 Special topics, A-Z
5169 Other regions or countries, A-Z

Alcoholism and religion
5175 General works
Alcoholism and the Bible
5180 General works
5182 Biblical argument against wines, etc.
5183 Biblical argument in favor of wines, etc.
5184 Communion wines
5185 Alcoholism and Judaism
Alcoholism and Christianity
Cf. BV4399, Alcoholism among the clergy
5186 General works
By region or country
5187 United States
5189 Other
Alcoholism and Christian missions
5194 General works
5197 By region or country, A-Z
.5 Alcoholism and Islam
Alcoholism and native races
5198 General works
5199 By region or country, A-Z
Under each country:
.X General works
.x2 Local, A-Z
5200 Alcoholism in colonies and in the tropics
5201 Other topics, A-Z
.A4 Aircraft drinking
.S6 Social aspects of drinking in bars, etc.

Women and temperance reform
5203 Periodicals. Serials
Prefer HV5285, HV5301+, subdivision (1) under each country, when in doubt
5207 Handbooks, manuals, etc.
5209 Societies
5211 Congresses
5213 General works. History

Alcoholism. Intemperance. Temperance reform
Women and temperance reform - Continued
Biography
Cf. HV5030+, Alcoholism
HV5232, Women and temperance reform
HV5293, Intemperance
HV5301+, Alcoholism by region or country
5215 Collective
5218 Individual, A-Z
By region or country
United States
5221 Periodicals. Serials
5225 Handbooks, manuals, etc.
5227 Societies
5228 Congresses. Conventions
5229 General works. History
5232 Biography of reformers, A-Z
Cf. HV5030+, Alcoholism
HV5215+, Women and temperance reform
HV5293, Intemperance
5235 By region or state, A-Z
Under each state:
.x General works
.x2 By city, A-Z
Other regions or countries
Under each country:
.x General works
.x2 Local, A-Z
5239 Canada
5241 Other American regions or countries, A-Z
5244 Europe. By region or country, A-Z
5247 Other. By region or country, A-Z
Pro-alcohol
5251 General works
By region or country
5253 United States
5255 Other regions or countries, A-Z
5258 Moderate drinking vs. total abstinence
Public house reform and substitutes for the saloon
5261 General works
By region or country
United States
5264 General works
5267 By region or state, A-Z
5268 By city, A-Z
5269 Other regions or countries, A-Z
Under each country:
.x General works
.x2 Local, A-Z
5271 Light wines, beer, etc. and temperance beverages
Care and rehabilitation of alcoholics
Including social work
Cf. RC525+, Alcoholic psychoses
RC565, Drug abuse
5275 General works
Practice. Methods of treatment
5276 General works
5277 Keeley cure
5278 Other special treatments (not A-Z)

Alcoholism. Intemperance. Temperance reform
Care and rehabilitation of alcoholics - Continued
By region or country
Including asylums and institutions
United States
5279 General works
5280 By region or state, A-Z
Including state institutions
5281 By place, A-Z
Including institutions other than state
5283 Other regions or countries, A-Z
Under each country:
.x General works
.x2 By place, A-Z

By region or country
United States
5285 Periodicals. Serials
5286 Yearbooks
5287 Societies
Class here general only; for state and local, see HV5297+
Subarranged like HS1510
5288 Congresses. Conferences
Collections
Documents
Cf. HV5076+, Federal documents
HV5298, City documents
5289.A1-49 Serial
.A5 Special. By date
.A7-Z Nonofficial collections
5290 Dictionaries. Encyclopedias
General works. History
5291 Early through 1860
5292 1861-
5293 Biography
Cf. HV5030+, Alcoholism
HV5215+, Women and temperance reform
HV5232, Biography of reformers
Reform literature
Including addresses, essays, lectures, sermons
5295 Early through 1860
5296 1861-
5297 By region or state, A-Z
5298 By city, A-Z
Including reports of license commissioners, etc.

Alcoholism. Intemperance. Temperance reform

By region or country - Continued

5301-5720.5 Other regions or countries. Table IX 1/

Under each country:

10 nos.	5 nos.	2 nos.	1 no.	
(1)	(1)		.A1-5	Periodicals. Serials
(2)				Yearbooks
(3)	(2)			Societies
(4)				Congresses. Conferences
(5)				Collections
				.A1-5 Documents
				Cf. HV5080, Alcoholism and the state
				.A1-49 Serial
				.A5 Special. By date
				.A7-Z Nonofficial collections
(6)	(3)	(1)	.A6-Z7	General works. History
(7)				Biography
				Cf. HV5030+, Alcoholism HV5215+, Women and temperance reform HV5232+, Alcoholism by region or country
(8)	(4)			Reform literature
				.A3 Early
		(2)		Local, A-Z
(9)	(5).A3		.Z8	By state, A-Z
(10)				By city, A-Z

Tobacco habit

Cf. GT3020, Manners and customs

RC567, Drug abuse

5725	Periodicals. Serials
5726	Societies
5727	Collected works (nonserial)
5730	History
	Biography
5731	Collective
.5	Individual, A-Z
	General works
5732	Scientific
5733	Popular reform literature
5735	Other general (not A-Z)
	Special topics
5740	Cigarette smoking
5745	Juvenile use of tobacco
5747	Tobacco and the clergy
5748	Other special
5751	Pro-tobacco
	For "Nicotiana," see GT3020

1/ For Table IX, see pp. 135-144. Add country number in table to 5300

Tobacco habit - Continued
By region or country
United States
5755 Societies
Collections
5756 Documents
5758 Nonofficial collections
5760 General works. History
5763 Reform literature
5765 Other
Local
5767 By region or state, A-W
5768 By city, A-Z
5770 Other regions or countries, A-Z
Under each country:
.x General (Documents, etc.)
.X2 Other

Drug habits. Drug abuse
Class here works on the social aspect of drug habits and drug abuse; for works on the medical aspects of drug abuse, see RC563+
For drug abuse and employment, see HF5549.5.D7
For police investigation of narcotics traffic, see HV8079.N3
5800 Periodicals. Societies. Serials
5801 General works
5804 Dictionaries. Encyclopedias
5805 Biography, A-Z
Study and teaching
5808 General works
.5 Audiovisual aids
5809 Research
Special
Class here only general works; for special regions or countries, see HV5825+
5810 Cocaine
5813 Morphine and chloral
5816 Opium
5819 Patent medicines
5822 Other, A-Z
.A5 Amphetamines
.B3 Barbiturates

.C3 Cannabis
.G4 Glue
.H25 Hallucinogenic drugs
.H3 Hashish

.H4 Heroin
.I8 Isonipecaine
.L9 Lysergic acid diethylamide (LSD)

.M3 Marihuana
.P45 Phencyclidine
.Q3 Qat

Drug habits. Drug abuse - Continued
5824 Drugs and special classes of persons, A-Z
Automobile drivers, see HE5620.D65
.E85 Ethnic minorites
.I5 Infants

Military personnel, see UH630
Minorities, see .E85
Prisoners, see HV8836.5
Prostitutes, see HQ120
.W6 Women

.Y67 Young men
.Y68 Youth

By region or country
For works on special classes of persons in particular places, see HV5824
United States
Including insular possessions
5825 General works
5831 By state, territory or insular possession, A-Z
Under each state:
Documents
.A1-3 Serials
.A5 Special. By date
.A6-Z Monographs
5833 By city, A-Z
5840 Other regions or countries, A-Z
Under each country:
General works
.xA1-5 Documents
.xA6-Z Other
.x2 Local, A-Z

CRIMINOLOGY

Periodical. Serials
Including scientific and anthropological serials
6001 English
6002 French
6003 German
6004 Italian
6005 Other
6006 Yearbooks
6008 Societies (International)
6010 Congresses (International)
6011 Exhibitions. Museums
Collected works (nonserial)
6015 Collected works of individual authors
6016 Other

Criminology - Continued
6017 Encyclopedias. Dictionaries
History of the science
6018 Theory, method. Statsitics (as a method)
6021 General works
6023 Biography. Criminologists
6024 Study and teaching
.5 Research
6025 General works
6028 Addresses, essays, lectures
6030 General special (Special aspects of the subject as a whole)

Criminal anthropology
For general form divisions, see HV6001+
For theory, method, see HV6018
For history of the science, see HV6021
General works
6035 English
6036 French
6037 German
6038 Italian
6039 Other
6041 Criminal anthropology and criminal law
The criminal type
6045 General works
6046 The delinquent woman
Cf. HQ1206+, Women's studies
6047 The born or instinctive criminal
6049 The habitual criminal. Recidivist
6051 The occasional criminal
6053 The criminal by passion
6054 Other
Anatomy. Physiognomy
6057 General works
Special
6059 Skull and brain
6061 Other
Criminal anthropometry
Cf. GN51+, Philosophy of anthropometry
6065 General works
Special
Bertillon method
6068 General works
6071 Photography of criminals
Cf. TR822, Photography in criminology and law
6074 Finger prints
6078 Other special (not A-Z)
6079 Forms, blanks, etc.
Criminal psychology
6080 General works
6083 Criminal responsibility
Cf. HV5055, Responsibility of alcoholics
6084 Psychology of the criminal crowd. The mass
Cf. HM281+, Social psychology
HV6107, Contagion of crime

Criminology
Criminal anthropology
Criminal psychology - Continued
Language of criminals
6085 General works
Slang, argot, see P
Dictionaries, see P
6089 Prison psychology
Intellectual and aesthetic characteristics
6093 General works
6097 Prison literature. Wall inscriptions
6098 Tattooing
6099 Other
Emotional and moral characteristics
6105 General works
6107 Contagion of crime. The "criminal pair," etc.
Cf. HV6084, Psychology of the criminal crowd
6110 Hypnotism and crime
Examination of exceptional criminals
6112 General and collective
6113 Special, A-Z
e. g. .L4 Leopold, Nathan
.L6 Loeb, Richard
Causes of crime. Criminal etiology
6115 Treatises. Theory
6117 Minor works. Nonsystematic works
6118 Primitive conceptions. Fall of man. Dualism
Freedom of the will, etc.
Cf. BF620+, Psychology
BJ1460+, Ethics
Heredity
6121 General works
6123 Atavism and degeneration
Cf. HV4987, Degeneration
6125 Family degeneration
Cf. HV4987, Degeneration
Influence of disease
6131 General works
6133 Psychopathology and crime. Insanity and crime
6143 Other
e. g. Endocrinology
Alcoholism and crime, see HV5053
Environment
6150 General works
Cosmic influences. Climate, etc.
6152 General works
6153 Local. By region or country, A-Z
No subarrangement by place
Social and domestic relations
6155 General works
6157 Family
6158 Sex
6163 Age
6166 Education
6168 Literature and the press
6169 Other

Criminology
Criminal anthropology
Causes of crime. Criminal etiology
Environment - Continued
Economic conditions
6171 General works
6172 The financial criminal
Cf. HV6763+, Financial crime
Insurance and crime, see HG8141; HG8938
6174 Pauperism and crime
Cf. HV4023+, Poor in cities
6177 Habitat. Crowding of population. Cities
Tenements
Cf. HD7285+, Housing
6181 Immigration and crime
6184 Other
6187 Political conditions and crime
6188 Military service and crime
6189 War and crime
6190 Other special
e. g. Automobiles and crime

Criminal ethnography. Race. Nationality
6191 General works
6194 By race, A-Z
e. g. Indians (North America), see E98.C87
.J4 Jews
6197 By region or country, A-Z
Under each country.
.x General works
.x2 Local, A-Z
Criminal classes
For customs relative to criminals and the underworld see GT6550+
6201 Periodicals. Serials
6205 Documents
6208 Statistics
General works. History and description
6211 General. Collections
e. g. Pitaval
By period
Ancient
6213 General works
Orient
6215 General works
6216 Assyria-Babylonia
6217 Egypt
6218 Other
Classic Occident
6219 General works
6221 Greece
6224 Rome
6227 Other
Medieval
6231 General works
Special with country, see HV6801+

Criminology
Criminal classes
General works. History and description
By period - Continued
Modern
6233 General works
6235 18th century
6239 19th century
6241 20th century
Biography
Cf. HV6211, Criminal classes
HV6278, Assassinations of rulers
HV6653, Biography of thieves
HV6766, Financial crime
HV6785, Crimes and offenses
HV6801+, Crimes and criminal classes
Subdivision (5) or (2), under each region or country, Collective biography
6245 Collective
6248 Individual, A-Z
For prison diaries, see HV9441+
6249 Crime in literature
e. g. Dickens
Cf. HV8655, Prisons in literature
By region or country, see HV6774+
Victims of crimes. Victimology
For works on victims of specific crimes or offenses, see the crime or offense, e. g. Murder, see HV6499+
6250 Periodicals. Serials
.2 Congresses
.25 General works
.3 By region or country, A-Z
For works on special classes of persons as victims in particular places, see HV6250.4
.4 Special classes of persons as victims, A-Z
.A34 Aged
.E75 Ethnic minorities
.G57 Girls
.S78 Students
.W65 Women
Crimes and offenses
General form divisions, see HV6201+
6251 General works
6253 Classification of crimes. Nomenclature
Political crimes
Class here only theory and psychology of political crimes; for descriptive works, history, politics, cases, see D, HJ, JF-JX, K, as the case may be
Offenses against the government
6254 General works
International (Breach of neutrality, piracy, etc.) see JX; for unauthorized negotiations, see JX1670

Criminology
Crimes and offenses
Political crimes
Offenses against the government - Continued
National
6273 General works
6275 Treason. Conspiracy
6278 Assassination of rulers. Regicide
Cf. HV6499+, Homicide
HX821+, Anarchism
6281 Other
By region or country
United States
6285 General works
6288 By region or state, A-W
6289 By city, A-Z
6295 Other regions or countries, A-Z
Under each country:
.x General works
.x2 Local, A-Z

Offenses against the administration, election laws, etc.
Class here only theory and psychology; for descriptive works, history, cases, etc., see D, HJ, JF-JX, K as the case may be
6301 General works
By region or country
United States
General
Documents
6303.A1-5 Federal
.A5-W State
6304 General works. History
6305 Other
Administration
6306 Bribery of officials. Venality in office
6308 Graft
6310 City and state "rings"
6312 Land steals
Cf. HD226, Land claims
Elections
6314 Bribery of voters
6316 Illegal voting

6321 Other regions or countries, A-Z
Under each country:
.x General works
.x2 Special topics (not A-Z)
.x3 Local, A-Z

Criminology
Crimes and offenses - Continued
Offenses against justice
Cf. note prefixed to HV6254
HV6455+, Lnyching
6323 General works
6325-6335 By region or country
United States
6325 General works
6326 Subornation or perjury, etc.
6327 Judicial corruption, etc.
Contempt of court, see JK1543
6329 Other
Local
6331 United States Federal cases. By date
6333 By region or state, A-Z
6334 By city, A-Z
Under each state and city use ".Z6" for cases by date
6335 Other regions or countries, A-Z
Under each country:
.x General works
.x2 Special. By topic (as in HV6326+)
Use .1-9 combined with number for region or country
.x3 Local. By place, A-Z
Offenses against the revenue
Cf. HG1+, Finance
HJ1+, Public finance
6337 General works
Counterfeiting, see HG335+
Smuggling, see HJ6690+
Illicit distilling, etc., see HJ5021
6351 Other
Offenses against postal laws, see HE6091+
Offenses against public health, see RA
Offenses against public safety
Cf. HD1+, Economic history
T1+, Technology
6419 General works
Offensive and dangerous industries, see HD3623+
Dangerous structures, etc., see TH219+, TH439+
6429 Other
Terrorism
6431 General works
By region or country
6432 United States
6433 Other regions or countries, A-Z
Offenses against the public order
6435 General works
Illegal organizations
Gangs
6437 General works
6439 By region or country, A-Z
Under each country:
.x General works
.x2 Local, A-Z

Criminology
Crimes and offenses
Offenses against the public order
Illegal organizations - Continued
Outlaws. Brigands. Feuds
e. g. Camorra, Mafia, Molly Maguires, Dacoits
6441 General works
By region or country
United States
6444 Documents
6446 General works. History and description
6448 Other
6452 By region or state, A-Z
Under each state:
.x General works
.x2 Special bands or feuds, A-Z
Subarranged by date
6453 Other regions or countries, A-Z
Under each country:
.x General works
.x2 By state or province, A-Z
.x3 Special bands, A-Z
Subarranged by date
Lynching
6455 General works
6457-6471 By region or country
United States
6457 General works. History, etc.
6458 Statistics
6459 Other
By region or country
Under each country:
.x General works
.x2 By region or state, A-Z
6461-6462 North. Central states
6464-6465 South. Southwest
6467-6468 West. Northwest
6471 Other regions or countries, A-Z
Under each country:
.x General works
.x2 Local, A-Z
Riots and unlawful assemblies. Mobs
Cf. HM281+, Crowds
HV6084, Psychology of the criminal crowd
6474 General works
By region or country
United States
6477 General works
6481 By region or state, A-Z
6483 By place, A-Z
6485 Other regions or countries, A-Z
Under each country:
.x General works
Local
.x2A1A-Z States and provinces
.x2A2-Z By place

Criminology
Crimes and offenses
Offenses against the public order - Continued
Disorderly conduct. Unnecessary noises
6486 General works
By region or country
United States
6488 General works
6489 By region or state, A-Z
6490 By place, A-Z
6491 Other regions or countries, A-Z
Under each country:
.x General works
.x2 Local, A-Z
6492 Other, A-Z
e. g. .C5 Concealed weapons
Crimes against the person
Class here only theory, psychology and and social aspects; for legal aspects, see K
Cf. HQ809+, Family violence
6493 General works

Homicide. Murder, etc.
Cf. HV6278, Regicide
R726, Euthanasia
6499 Collected works (nonserial)
History
6505 General works
6507 Ancient
6509 Medieval
Modern
6511 General works
6513 19th-20th centuries
6515 General works
By region or country
United States
6518 Documents
6521 Collected works (nonserial)
6524 History
Biography, see HV6245+
6528 Statistics
6529 General works
6533 By region or state, A-Z
6534 By city, A-Z
6535 Other regions or countries, A-Z
Under each country:
.x General works
.x2 By region, state or province, A-Z
.x3 By city, A-Z

Criminology
Crimes and offenses
Crimes against the person - Continued
Infanticide
6537 General works
Abortion, see HQ767
By region or country
6539 Non-Christian regions or countries, A-Z
Under each country:
.x General works
.x2 Local, A-Z
6541 Other regions or countries
Under each country:
.x General works
.x2 Local, A-Z
6542 Other special
e. g. Filicide, parricide, matricide, uxoricide
Suicide
Cf. HB1323.S8, Demography
RA1136, State medicine
General works. History, etc.
6543 Ancient
6544 Medieval and early modern through 1800
6545 1801-
6546 Suicide among special classes of persons
e. g. Children, prisoners, youth
6548 By region or country, A-Z
Under each country:
.x General works
.x2 Local, A-Z
Poisoning and poisoners
6549 General works. History, etc.
6551 Ancient
6552 Medieval and early modern through 1800
6553 1801-
6555 By region or country, A-Z
Under each country:
.x General works
.x2 Local, A-Z
Sex crimes, see HQ71+

Rape
Cf. RC560.R36, Psychiatric aspects
6558 General works
By region or country
United States
6561 General works
By region
6563 Southern states
Cf. HV6464+, Lynching
6564 Other regions, A-Z
6565 By state, A-W
6568 By place, A-Z
6569 Other regions or countries, A-Z
Under each country:
.x General works
.x2 Local, A-Z

Criminology
Crimes and offenses
Crimes against the person - Continued
Abduction
6571 General works
6574 By region or country, A-Z
Seduction
6584 General works
6587 By region or country, A-Z
6589 By case, A-Z
Kidnapping
6595 General works
By region or country
United States
6598 General works
6601 By region or state, A-Z
6602 By place, A-Z
6603 By case, A-Z
6604 Other regions or countries, A-Z
Under each country:
General
.xA1-3 Nonofficial serials
.xA4-5 Documents
.xA5 Separate documents. By date
.xA6-Z General works
.x2 By case, A-Z
6608 Mayhem
6618 Bodily assault
6626 Other
e. g. Wife beating
Crimes against reputation or honor
6629 General works
6631 Libel and slander
Cf. PN4888.C6, Corruption of the press
Z657, Liberty of the press
6632 Anonymous letters
Crimes against property
Class here only theory, psychology and social aspects; for legal aspects, see K
6635 General works
6638 Arson
Cf. HV8079.A7, Arson investigation
Piracy, see JX4444+
Theft
Including burglary, train and highway robbery, and horse stealing
Cf. HF5549.5.E43, Employee theft
HV6172, The financial criminal
HV6763+, Financial crime
HV9067.S7, Stealing (Juvenile)
TH9701+, Burglar proof construction, alarm equipment, etc.
6646 Collected works (nonserial)
General works. History and description
6648 General works
6649 Ancient
6650 Modern
6651 19th century
6652 20th century

Criminology
Crimes and offenses
Crimes against property
Theft - Continued
6653 Biography of thieves
Cf. HV6245+, Biography of criminals
By region or country
United States
6658 General works
6661 By region or state, A-Z
Under each state:
.x General works
.x2 Cases. By date of crime
6665 Other regions or countries, A-Z
Under each country:
.x General works
.x2 Cases. By date
Embezzlement. Forgery, etc.
6675 General works
By region or country
United States
6679 General works
6684 By place, A-Z
6685 Other regions or countries, A-Z
Under each country:
.x General works
.x2 By place, A-Z
6688 Extortion
Frauds. "Bunco-games," etc.
Cf. HG8141, Insurance crimes
6691 General works
By region or country
United States
6693 Collected works (nonserial)
6695 General works. History and description
6697 Other
6698 By place, A-Z
.Z9A-Z Cases
6699 Other regions or countries, A-Z
Under each country:
.x General works
.x2 Local, A-Z
6700 Humbugs, quacks, etc.
Offenses against public morals
Cf. HQ101+, Prostitution
HV5001+, Alcoholism, tobacco and drug habits
K, Law
6705 General works
6707 By region or country, A-Z
Gambling
Including legal aspects of racetrack gambling, etc.
Cf. GV1247, Card sharping
GV1301+, Chance and banking games
HG4626, Bucket shops
HG6001+, Speculation
6708 Collected works (nonserial)
6710 General works. History

Criminology
Crimes and offenses
Offenses against public morals
Gambling - Continued
6713 Other
e. g. Reform
By region or country
United Staters
6715 General works
6718 Horse racing
Cf. SF331, Betting
6721 By place, A-Z
6722 Other regions or countries, A-Z
Under each country:
.x General works
.x2 Special topics, A-Z
Cf. HV6718, Horse racing
.x3 By place, A-Z
Lotteries, see HG6105+
6727 Obscene literature
Cf. HQ291+, Social purity
HQ471, Pornography
Malpractice, see RA1056.5
Grave robbing, see RA641
6733 Prize fighting
Cf. GV1111+, Human fighting
Dueling, see CR4571+
6738 Other, A-Z
e. g. .H6 Sale of honors
Imposture
Ct. BR718, Religious imposters
CT9980+, Biographies of imposters, impersonators, etc.
D107.6, Biographies of pretenders
6751 General works. History and description
Literary forgeries, see PN171
6757 Other
By region or country
United States
6759 General works
6760 Cases, A-Z
6761 Other regions or countries, A-Z
Under each country:
.x General works
.x2 Cases, A-Z
Missing persons
6762.A3A-Z General works
.A4-Z By region or country, A-Z
Financial crime
Cf. HV6172, The financial criminal
HV6635+, Crimes against property
6763 Collected works (nonserial)
6765 History
6766 Biography, A-Z
Cf. HV6245+, General biography of criminals
6768 General works

Criminology
Crimes and offenses
Financial crime - Continued
By region or country
United States
6769 General works
6770.A2 By region or state, A-W
.A4-Z By city
6771 Other regions or countries, A-Z
Under each country:
.x General works
Local
.x2A2A-Z By state or province
.x2A6-Z By place
6773 Other, A-Z
Debt, see HV8650+
Extortion, see HV6688

Crimes and criminal classes
Class here general works and works not limited to one or two special subjects
By region or country
United States
Periodicals, serials, see HV6201
6774 Societies. Associations for prevention of crime
Cf. HV7431, Prevention of crime
Collections
6775 Documents
6777 Other
History
6779 General works
6781 Early
6783 19th-20th centuries
6785 Biography (Collective)
For individual, see HV6248
6786 Portraits and descriptions of criminals and escaped prisoners. "Rogues' galleries."
6787 Statistics
6789 General works
6791 General special
e. g. Interstate compacts, rural crime
6793 By region or state, A-Z
6795 By place, A-Z

Criminology
Crimes and criminal classes
By region or country - Continued

6801-7220.5 Other regions or countries. Table IX 1/
Under each country:

10 nos.	5 nos.	2 nos.	1 no.	
	(1)		.A1-5	Collections
(1)				Documents
(2)				Other
		(1)		General works
(3)	(2)			History
	.A01-26			General
	.A3-5			By period Subarranged, A-Z
(4)	.A6-Z5			Recent
(5)	.Z6A-Z			Biography (Collective) For individual, see HV6248
(6)	(3)			Statistics
(7)			.A6-Z7	General works
		(2)		Local, A-Z
(9)	(4)		.Z8	By state, province, etc., A-Z
(10)	(5)			By place, A-Z

PENOLOGY

Class here detection and punishment of crime; reformation of offenders

Cf. HV6001+, Criminology
HV8301+, Prisons. Penitentiaries. Punishment and reform

Periodicals. Serials
7231 English
7232 French
7233 German
7234 Italian
7239 Other

Societies (International). Associations (International)
7240 General works
7241 Proceedings, etc. By date
7242 International Penal and Prison Commission

1/ For Table IX, see pp. 135-144. Add country number in table to 6800

Penology - Continued
7243 Congresses (International)
7244 Museums. Exhibitions
Documents
Including administration of justice and criminal statistics
United States
Mainly confined to statistics
Federal
7245 Serial
7248 Nonserial. By date
State
Under each:
.A1-5 Serial
.A6 Nonserial. By date
.A7-Z By place, A-Z
7250 Alabama
7251 Alaska
7252 Arizona
7253 Arkansas
7254 California
7255 Colorado
7256 Connecticut
Dakota Territory, see HV7291
7257 Delaware
7258 District of Columbia
7259 Florida
7260 Georgia
.5 Hawaii
7261 Idaho
7262 Illinois
7263 Indian Territory
7264 Indiana
7265 Iowa
7266 Kansas
7267 Kentucky
7268 Louisiana
7269 Maine
7270 Maryland
7271 Massachusetts
7272 Michigan
7273 Minnesota
7274 Mississippi
7275 Missouri
7276 Montana
7277 Nebraska
7278 Nevada
7279 New Hampshire
7280 New Jersey
7281 New Mexico
7282 New York
7283 North Carolina
7284 North Dakota
7285 Ohio
7286 Oklahoma
7287 Oregon
7288 Pennsylvania
7289 Rhode Island

Penology
Documents
United States
State - Continued
7290 South Carolina
7291 South Dakota
7292 Tennessee
7293 Texas
7294 Utah
7295 Vermont
7296 Virginia
7297 Washington
7298 West Virginia
7299 Wisconsin
7300 Wyoming
7315-7400 Other regions or countries. Table I/
Under each country:
.A1-5 Periodicals. Serials
.A6 Nonserial. By date
.A7-Z8 By region or state, A-Z
.A9A-Z By city, A-Z

Collections of monographs, essays, etc.
7405 Several authors
7407 Individual authors
7411 Dictionaries. Encyclopedias
Statistics (Monographs)
For serial documents, see HV7245+
Cf. HV8482+, Statistics (Serial)
7415 General works
7418 Forms. Blanks for statistics, etc.
Treatises, see HV8661+
7428 Social work with delinquents and criminals
7431 Prevention of crime, methods, etc.
e. g. Organization and working of societies for the prevention and prosecution of crime; for their publications, reports, etc., see HV6774+
By region or country, see HV9441+

1/ For Table I, see p. 135-144. Add country number in table to 7300

Penology - Continued
Police. Detectives. Constabulary
7551 Periodicals. Serials
Societies, see HV7240+
Congresses, see HV7243
Exhibitions, see HV7244
Documents
Including administrative, etc.
7561-7895 By region or country
7561-7625 United States
Federal (Secret service)
Cf. HV7961, National police
7561 General works
7565 Special. By date
7568 Commission reports, etc.
Directories, see HV8130
7571 By region or state, A-Z
Under each state:
.x General works
.x2 Special. By date
.x3 Commission reports, etc.
.x4 By county, parish, etc., A-Z
District of Columbia, see HV7619
7575-7625 City
For reports of departments of public safety, including fire, police, and in some cases, other departments, see JS13, unless some special reason appears to the contrary
Under each:
.A Report of the department
.B-C Bureau reports
.D3 Special reports. By date
.E3 Commissions. Investigations
.K Regulations
.Q Manual. By date
.S Directories. By date
If combined with manual, see subdivision Q
7575 A to Baltimore
7576 Baltimore
7577 Baltimore to Boston
7578 Boston
7579 Boston to Brooklyn
7580 Brooklyn
7583 Brooklyn to Chicago
7584 Chicago
7585 Chicago to Cincinnati
7586 Cincinnati
7595 Cincinnati to New York
7597 New York
7599 New York to Philadelphia
7601 Philadelphia
7603 Philadelphia to Pittsburgh
7605 Pittsburgh
7607 Pittsburgh to Q
7608 R to St. Louis

Penology
  Police. Detectives. Constabulary
    Documents
      By region or country
        United States
          City - Continued

7609	St. Louis
7612	St. Louis to San Francisco
7613	San Francisco
7618	San Francisco to Washington
7619	Washington Including District of Columbia
.T3	Capitol police
7625	Washington to Z
7641-7895	Other regions or countries. Table III 1/ Under each country: 3 nos. (1) Ministry or department .A1-5 General works .A6 Special. By date .A8 Commission reports. Investigations, etc. By date .K Regulations .Q Manuals (2) State, A-Z (3) City, A-Z If only two numbers are available, use 2.5 for city Under each: .A Report of the department .B-C Bureau reports .D3 Special reports. By date .E3 Commission reports. Investigations .K Regulations .Q Manuals .S Directories, etc. 1 no. .A2A-Z General works .A5-Z Local, A-Z
7897	Collected works (nonserial)
7899	Minor works. Collected pamphlets
7900	Directories
7901	Dictionares. Encyclopedias
	History
7903	General works
7906	Early through 1800
7909	1801-

1/ For Table III, see pp. 135-144. Add country number in table to 7600

Penology
Police. Detectives. Constabulary - Continued
Biography
7911.A1 Collective
.A2-Z Individual, A-Z
Police and detective narratives
Cf. HV6211, History and description of criminal classes
7914 English
7915 French
7916 German
7917 Other
7921 General works, treatises, and advanced textbooks
Cf. HV8661+, Treatises on forms of punishment
7922 Juvenile works
7923 Study and teaching (General)
Cf. HV7561+, Secret service
HV8130+, Police by region or country
7924 Ethics
Law, see K
Administration and organization
7935 General works
.5 Police psychology. Psychological aspects of police work
7936 Special topics, A-Z
.A8 Automation. Electronic data processing
Chaplains, see BV4375.5
.C75 Collective bargaining
.C79 Communication
.C8 Communication systems
Correspondence, see .R4
.C85 Corruption
.D5 Discipline
.D54 Discretion
Electronic data processing, see .A8
.E7 Equipment and supplies
.H4 Health and hygiene
Lockouts, see .S75
.M4 Medals
.P47 Personnel management
.P7 Productivity
.P75 Psychologists and psychiatrists
.P8 Public relations
Cf. PN4901+, Police and the press
.R4 Records and correspondence
.R5 Recruiting
.R53 Reports
.S56 Shooting ranges
.S75 Strikes and lockouts
.S8 Supervision of police personnel
.T4 Television
.V3 Police vehicle location systems
.V4 Police vehicles

Penology
Police. Detectives. Constabulary
Administration and organization - Continued
National police. Constabulary. Gendarmes
7938 General works
Administration
7941 General works
7943 Minister of police
7945 National bureau
7948 Other
Organization
7951 General works
Revenue service, see HJ
Constabulary and frontier police
7955 General works
7957 Mounted police
7959 Game and forest police
7961 Secret service
Cf. HV7561+, Police documents
HV8141, Police policy and methods
HV8157+, (Subdivision 2), Police by region or country
7963 Other
7964 Colonial police
For individual corps, see the specific area in HV8157+
State and county. Rural police. Sheriffs, etc.
7965 General works
Administration
Commissioners. Boards of control
7967 General works
7969 State
7971 County
7973 Relation to state and county courts
Cf. K, Law
Organization
7977 General works
7979 Sheriffs
7981 Deputies and constables
7983 Bailiffs
7985 Other
Municipal police. Town constables
7988 General works
Administration. Commissions and boards of control
7991 General works
Including public safety in general
Police relations
7992 General works
7993 The public
7994 The city government
7995 The courts
Cf. Class K, Law
7996 The criminal classes
7997 Other
7999 Other

Penology
Police. Detectives. Constabulary
Administration and organization
Municipal police. Town constables - Continued
Organization
8001 General works
8002 Discipline
8003 Physical requirements
8005 Civil service
8007 Tactics, uniforms, etc.
8009 Other
Officials. Personnel
8012 Chief
8014 Minor officers
8016 Patrolmen
Mounted police
8018 General works
8019 Bicycle police
8021 Police detectives
8023 Policewomen
8025 Other
e. g. Police dogs, radio
Railway police, see HE1771
Airport police, see HE9797.4.P6
Police duty. Methods of protection
8031 General works
Special classes of crimes, offenses, and criminals
Cf. HV6251+, Crimes and offenses
HV9051+, Juvenile delinquency
Provision against political crimes and criminals
8035 General works
8037 Provision against anarchists
8039 Provision against election disorders and illegal voting
8041 Protection of courts of justice, etc.
Protection of mails, postal service, etc., see HE6091+
Protection of public health, accidents, see RA
8049 Preservation of public safety
Provision against illegal organization and assemblies
8053 General works
8055 Suppression of riots
8057 Provision against homicide, etc.
8058 Provision against kidnapping, etc.
8059 Regulation of sale and use of firearms, knives, etc.
8061 Protection of property against theft, etc.
8065 Protection against fraud, etc.
8067 Protection of public morals
Cf. HQ101+, Prostitution, etc.
HV5001+, Alcoholism, etc.
8069 Other
e. g. Provision against racial crimes

Penology
Police. Detectives. Constabulary
Police duty. Methods of protection - Continued
Investigation of crimes. Examination and identification of prisoners
Cf. K, Law
For documents, see HV7245+
8073 General works. Identification of persons. Forensic chemistry
Cf. RA1057, Medical jurisprudence
Bertillion method, see HV6068
Photography of criminals, see HV6071
Finger prints, see HV6074
.4 Composite drawings
.5 Other special
e. g. Voice
.8 Juvenile works
Identification of documents. Proof of handwriting
Cf. BF889+, Graphology
HV6675+, Forgery
8074 General works
8075 Typewritten documents
8076 Miscellaneous special
e. g. Ink
Identification of weapons
e. g. Firearms, forensic ballistics, etc.
8077 General works
Criminal photography, see TR822
.5 Identification of other objects, A-Z
.A98 Automobiles
.C6 Clothing
.T57 Tires
Medical jurisprudence (Expert testimony, cause of death, etc.), see RA1001+
Detection of lying
Cf. JK468.L5, Lie detectors. Polygraphs (United States)
8078.A1 Periodicals. Societies. Serials
.A2-Z General works
8079 Investigation and detection of special crimes, A-Z
.A7 Arson
Cf. HG9711+, Fire insurance
.B8 Burglary
.F7 Fraud
.H6 Homicide
.N3 Narcotics traffic
.O73 Organized crime
.W47 White collar crime
Police social work
Cf. BV4375.5, Police chaplains
8079.2 General works
.225 Services for the aged
.25 Services for juveniles

Penology
Police. Detectives. Constabulary
Police duty. Methods of protection - Continued

8079.5 Traffic control
.55 Traffic accident investigation
8080 Other police duties and methods of protection, A-Z
.A3 Aeronautics in police work
.A6 Arresting of suspects
Including physical methods

.D5 Disaster operations
.P2 Patrol
.P9 Pursuit driving

.R6 Roadblocks
.U5 Undercover operations

Coroner and coroner's courts, see K
Police justice, police courts, see K
Cf. HV7973, State and county courts
HV7995, Municipal police
Law, police codes, see K

Private detectives. Detective bureaus

8081 General works. History
Biography
Cf. HV7911+, Biography of police and police narratives
8083.A3 Collective
.A4-Z Individual, A-Z
8084 Policy. Abuses, etc.
8085 Handbooks, manuals, etc.
e. g. Brady, How to become a detective
By region or country
United States
8087 Agencies
e. g. Pinkerton's
8088 General works. History and description
Biography, see HV7911+
8091 Policy. Methods
Including abuses, spotters, etc.
8093 Handbooks, manuals, etc.
8095 Other
8096 By state, A-W
8097 By region or city, A-Z
8099 Other regions or countries, A-Z
Under each country:
.xA1-2 Periodicals. Societies
Documents
.xA3-4 Serials
.xA5 Nonserials. By date
.xA6-Z General works
.x2 By state or province, A-Z
.x3 By region or city, A-Z

Penology
Police. Detectives. Constabulary - Continued
Police
By region or country
United States
Periodicals, serials, see HV7551
Documents, see HV7561+
8130 Directories
8131 Collected works (nonserial)
8132 Congresses. Conventions. By date
8133 Dictionaries. Encyclopedias
General works. History and description
8135 Early
8138 19th-20th centuries
Biography, see HV7911
8141 Policy. Methods
Police and detective narratives, see HV7914
8143 Miscellany. Instruction, etc.
8145 By region or state, A-Z
8148 By city, A-Z
Under each:
.x General works. History and description
.x2 Other
8157-8280.7 Other regions or countries. Table V 1/
Under each country:

4 nos.	1 no.	
		Documents, see HV7641+
(1)	.A2A-Z	General works. History and description
(2)		Policy. Methods
		e. g. France - Lettres de cachet
		Local
(3)	.A5	By region or state, A-Z
(4)	.A6-Z	By city, A-Z

8290 Guards. Watchmen
Including protection of factories, public buildings, etc.
Cf. HF5549.5.E43, Employee theft
TH9701+, Burglar proof construction, alarm equipment, etc.
For protection of classified defense information in industry, see UB249
Prisons. Penitentiaries. Punishment and reform
8301 Periodicals. Serials (published by prisoners)
Societies, associations, see HV7241+, (International) and HV8967 (Reform)
Congresses, see HV7243, International congresses
Documents
Class here reports of prisons, etc.
United States
Federal
8311 Serial
8314 Nonserial. By date
8317 Commissions. Investigations. By date

1/ For Table V, see pp. 135-144. Add country number in table to 8150

Penology
Prisons. Penitentiaries. Punishment and reform
Documents
United States - Continued
State
Class here state prisons
Under each:
(1) Serial
(2) Nonserial. By date
(3) Commissions. Investigations. By date

8320 Alabama
8321 Alaska
8322 Arizona
8323 Arkansas
8324 California
8325 Colorado
8326 Connecticut
Dakota Territory, see HV8361
8327 Delaware
8328 District of Columbia
8329 Florida
8330 Georgia
.5 Hawaii
8331 Idaho
8332 Illinois
8333 Indian Territory
8334 Indiana
8335 Iowa
8336 Kansas
8337 Kentucky
8338 Louisiana
8339 Maine
8340 Maryland
8341 Massachusetts
8342 Michigan
8343 Minnesota
8344 Mississippi
8345 Missouri
8346 Montana
8347 Nebraska
8348 Nevada
8349 New Hampshire
8350 New Jersey
8351 New Mexico
8352 New York
8353 North Carolina
8354 North Dakota
8355 Ohio
8356 Oklahoma
8357 Oregon
8358 Pennsylvania
8359 Rhode Island
8360 South Carolina
8361 South Dakota
8362 Tennessee
8363 Texas
8364 Utah

Penology
Prisons. Penitentiaries. Punishment and reform
Documents
United States
State - Continued

8365 Vermont
8366 Virginia
8367 Washington
8368 West Virginia
8369 Wisconsin
8370 Wyoming
8378 City. By city (including counties, etc.), A-Z
Under each:
.x Serial
.x2 Nonserial. By date
.x3 Commissions, investigations. By date
8395-8480 Other regions or countries. Table I 1/
Under each country:
.A1-5 Serial
.A6 Nonserial. By date
.A7-Z State institutions
8481 Forms. Blanks, etc. By region or country, A-Z
Encyclopedias. Dictionaries, see HV7411
Statistics (Serial)
Including statistics of institutions
For general criminal statistics, see HV7245+; HV7415
United States
8482.A1-4 General works
.A5-W States
8483 Canada
8484 Other American regions or countries, A-Z
8485 Europe. By region or country, A-Z
8486 Asia. By region or country, A-Z
8487 Africa. By region or country, A-Z
8488 Australia, A-Z
Collected works (nonserial)
8491 General
8493 Collected papers of individual authors
History and antiquities
8497 History of penal science
8501 General works
8505 Primitive
Ancient
8508 General works
Classic Orient
8511 Egypt
8513 Assyria
8515 Hebrews
8517 India
8519 China
8521 Japan
8523 Greece
8526 Rome

1/ For Table I, see pp. 135-144. Add country number in table to 8380

Penology
Prisons. Penitentiaries. Punishment and reform
History and antiquities - Continued
Medieval through 1800
8529 General works
8532 By region or country, A-Z
Modern
General works, see HV9441+
By region or country, see HV9456+

Forms of punishments (Early)
8545 General works
Modern forms of punishments, see HV8693
History, see HV8497+
Imprisonment and penal servitude, see HV8705+
Capital punishment
For modern treatises, modern modes of infliction, and controversial literature, see HV8694+
8551 General works
Beheading
8552 General works
8553 The headsman
8555 The guillotine
8558 Boiling in oil, etc.
8561 Breaking on the wheel
8564 Burning at the stake
8569 Crucifixion
8572 Drawing and quartering
8575 Drowning
Hanging
8579 General works
8581 Hanging in chains
8586 Pressing to death

Torture
Including judicial torture, "Putting the question," etc.
Cf. K, Law
8593 General works
8597 The rack
8599 By region or country, A-Z
8609 Mutilation. Branding
Flogging. Flagellation
Including general works dealing with religious penitence as well as other usages
For flogging in the army, see UB810+
For flogging in the navy, see VB910
8613 General works
Including curiosa
Cf. HQ79, Sadism. Masochism. Fetishism, etc.
8619 Whipping post
Cf. HV8772, Flogging
8621 By region or country, A-Z

Penology
Prisons. Penitentiaries. Punishment and reform
History and antiquities
Forms of punishments (Early)
Minor punishments
8623 General works
8626 Ducking stool. Cucking stool
8630 Penance
8633 Pillory
8637 Scold's bridle
8641 Stocks and jougs. Shackles
8644 Tarring
8646 Local. By region or country, A-Z
Galleys. Bagnios
Including prison hulks
8647 General works
8648 By region or country, A-Z
8649 Personal narratives
Other special
Debtors' prisons. Imprisonment for debt
8650 General works
8651 By region or country, A-Z
Sanctuaries. Cities of refuge
Including ancient and medieval aspects
8652 General works
8654 By region or country, A-z
Prisons in literature. Famous prisons
Class here only popular works
Cf. HV6249, Crime in literature
8655 General works
8656 Individual prisons. By region or country, A-Z
For scientific treatises, see HV9747+; HV9501+, subdivisions (9) and (10) or (4) and (5) under each country
Under each country:
(1) General works
(2) Individual prisons, A-Z
For political prisons, see class D
Biography of famous prisoners, famous escapes, etc.
Class here only popular works; for prison diaries, see HV9441+
Cf. HV6245+, Biography of criminals
8657 Collective
8658 Individual, A-Z
Cf. D285.8.C3+, Casanova
General works. Treatises
8661 Early through 1830
e. g. Beccaria
Modern
Cf. HV7921, Treatises on the police
8665 English and American
8666 French
8667 German
8669 Other languages (not A-Z)

Penology
Prisons. Penitentiaries. Punishment and reform - Continued

8670 Handbooks, manuals, etc.
Theory of punishment
8671 Early works
Modern theories
8675 General works
8681 Retaliation
8683 Retribution
8685 Reform
8686 Nonresistance to evil
Errors of criminal justice and their causes, see K
8688 Right to compensation for injury or loss through criminal activity
Cf. K, Law
Reparation for false arrest, prosecution, imprisonment
8689 General works
8691 By region or country, A-Z
The pardoning power
Cf. JF265, Constitutional history
8692 General works
By region or country, see HV9441+

Forms of punishment (Modern)
For early, see HV8551+
8693 General works
Capital punishment
8694 Modern treatises
For earlier works, see HV8551+
8696 Modes of infliction
e. g. Electrocution, lethal gas
Cf. HV8545+, Earlier modes of infliction
HV8579, Hanging
Controversial literature
8697 Arguments in favor of capital punishment
8698 Arguments opposed to capital punishment
8699 By region or country, A-Z

Imprisonment. Penal servitude
8705 General works
8706 General special (Special aspects of the subject as a whole)
e. g. Fines vs. imprisonment
Terms of sentence
For serial documents, see HV8311+
8708 General works
8711 Life imprisonment
8713 Maximum and minimum term
8715 Indeterminate sentence
Probation, parole, see HV9278
8719 Other

Penology
Prisons. Penitentiaries. Punishment and reform
Forms of punishment (Modern)
Imprisonment. Penal servitude - Continued
Systems of imprisonment
8723 General works
8726 Early
Including barracks, hulks, etc.
8728 Solitary system
8731 Silent or Auburn system
8733 Progressive system
8735 Other
8738 Prisons for women
Prisons for the insane
8741 General works
8742 By region or country, A-Z
Under each country:
.x General works
.x2 Special
Military prisons, see UB800+
Naval prisons, see VB890+
8745 Jails and houses of detention
For juvenile prisons, see HV9051+
Workhouses
Cf. HV69, Work relief
8748 General works
8749 By region or country, A-Z
Prison methods and practice
Prison psychology, see HV6089
Prison economy and discipline
8751 General works
For special countries, see HV9469; HV9501+, subdivision (6) or (3)
8754 Study and teaching. Research
Administration
8756 General works
8759 Organization of staff
8763 Other
e. g. Classification of prisoners, prison officials and records
8764 Self-government
Discipline of prisoners
8766 General works
Punishment of refractory prisoners
8769 General works
8772 Flogging
8775 Treadmill
8778 Other
Transporting and registering of prisoners
8788 General works
Transportation and carriage
8791 General works
8793 Prison registers
For identification, see HV6065+
8795 Other
By region or country
8797 United States
8799 Other regions or countries, A-Z

Penology
Prisons. Penitentiaries. Punishment and reform
Prison methods and practice - Continued
Systems of prison construction. Architecture, etc.
8805 General works
Plans
8808 General works
8811 Model prisons
8813 Cellular systems
8815 Site and situations
Heating and ventilation, see TH7392.P8
8819 Equipment and furnishing
8825 Other topics, A-Z
By region or country
United States
8827 General works
8828 States, A-W
8829 Other regions or countries, A-Z
Under each country:
.x General works
.x2 States, A-Z
Prison hygiene. Medical service
8833 General works
8835 Sanitation
8836 Sex in prison
.5 Drugs and prisoners
8837 Hospital service
For rehabilitation of chronic alcoholic offenders, see HV5275+
8841 Other
e. g. Physical training
Prison food. Diet
8845 General works
By region or country
United States
8847 General works
8848 Special
e. g. The steward's job
8849 Other regions or countries, A-Z
Costume of prisoners
8855 General works
8858 Special topics, A-Z
8860 Provision for recreation of prisoners
Provision for religious and moral instruction of prisoners (Administrative aspects)
Cf. BV4465, Christian work with prisoners
8865 General works
8867 The chaplain
8869 Other special (not A-Z)
Provision for education of prisoners
8875 General works
8878 Instruction in crafts or trades
8881 Prison libraries
Cf. Z675.P8, Library science
Z1039.P8, General bibliography
8883 Other special (not A-Z)

Penology
Prisons. Penitentiaries. Punishment and reform
Prison methods and practice - Continued

8883.5 Civil defense programs. Use of prisoners in disasters and civilian defense
8884 Provision for outside contacts of prisoners
e. g. Correspondence, visits
Cf. HV9278, Probation, parole
.5 Prison furloughs
Provision for prisoners' families
8885 General works
8886 By region or country, A-Z
8887 Release gratuities

Prison labor
History and policy
8888 General works
8891 Early. Disciplinary, unproductive labor
Cf. HV8647+, Galleys, bagnios
HV8775, Treadmill
8893 Prison labor vs. free labor
Cf. HD4861+, Slave, service and contract labor
8895 Other
8897 Theory. Treatises
8899 Minor works
Systems and method
8905 General works
8908 Contract labor
8911 Piece price system
8915 Public account system. State use
8918 Lease system
8921 Other
8923-8931 By region or country
United States
8923 Documents
.A1-59 Serial
.A6 Nonserial. By date
8925 General works. History and policy
8928 Other
8929 By region or state, A-Z
Under each state:
.x Documents
.x2 General works
8931 Other regions or countries, A-Z
Under each country:
.x General works
.x2 Local, A-Z

Penology
Prisons. Penitentiaries. Punishment and reform - Continued
Penal colonies. Transportation
8935 History and description
8938 Other general works
8941 Ticket of leave men
8943 Other
By region or country
e. g. Country of origin
Under each country:
(1) General
.A1-5 Documents
.A6-Z General works. History and policy
(2) By colony, A-Z

8945-8946 United States
8947 Other American regions or countries, A-Z
8949-8950 Great Britain
8955-8956 France
8959 Other European regions or countries, A-Z
8960 Asia. By region or country, A-Z
8961 Africa. By region or country, A-Z
8962 Australia and the Pacific islands, A-Z
Concentration camps. Internment camps
For camps arising out of war conditions, see the war, e. g. DP267.67, Spanish Civil War
8963 General works
8964 By region or country, A-Z
Prison reform
Class here works on theory and controversy; for descriptive material, practice, see HV9441+
Periodicals. Serials, see HV7231+
Societies (International), see HV7240+
Congresses (International), see HV7243
8971 Collections (International)
8975 History of the movement
Biography of reformers
8976 Collective
8978 Individual, A-Z
Reform literature
8980 Early through 1850
8982 1851-
Societies. Associations
8987 United States
8992 Other American regions or countries, A-Z
8995 Great Britain
9001 France
9006 Other European regions or countries, A-Z
9010 Asia. By region or country, A-Z
9014 Africa. By region or country, A-Z
9018 Australia and Pacific islands, A-Z
9025 Prison violence

Penology - Continued
The Juvenile offender. Juvenile delinquency.
Reform schools, etc.
Cf. HV7428, Social work with delinquents and criminals
LB3013.3, Violence in schools

9051	Periodicals. Serials
9055	Societies. Associations
9058	Congresses. Conventions
9061	Collected works (nonserial)
9064	Statistics: Theory, method, forms, blanks, etc.
9065	History
9067	By offense, A-Z e. g. .H6 Homicide .S7 Stealing
9068	Study and teaching. Schools
	General works, treatises, and advanced textbooks
9069	English
9071	French
9073	German
9076	Other
9076.5	Special topics (not A-Z) e. g. Comic books Cf. HV5135, Alcohol and youth
	Law, see K
9081	Education of delinquent children. Industrial training, etc. Cf. LC4801, Problem children
9082	Employment of delinquent children
9083	Physical education and sports for juvenile delinquents
	Parental correction
9085	General works
9086	Parental rights and the state
9101-9230.7	By region or country. Table V 1/ Under each country:

4 nos.	1 no.	
(1)	.A1-4	Periodicals. Societies. Serials
(2)	.A5A-Z	General works. History and policy
(3)	.A6	By region or state, A-Z
(4)	.A7-Z	By city, A-Z Under each: .x General works .x2 Institutions. By name, A-Z

1/ For Table V, see pp. 135-144. Add country number in table to 9100

Penology - Continued

Reformation and reclamation of adult prisoners

Including institutions for men, e. g. Elmira reformatory, and institutions for women

Cf. HQ301+, Rescue work

9261 Periodicals. Serials

9265 Associations. Prisoners' aid societies (International)

9267 Congresses

9272 History and policy

9274 Research

9275 General works

9276 General special (Special aspects of the subject as a whole)

9277 Payment of fines in instalments

9278 Probation. Parole

For reports of probation officers and courts, see HV9301+

Methods of assistance

9281 General works

9285 Education

9288 Employment

9301-9430.7 By region or country. Table V 1/

Under each country:

4 nos.	1 no.	
(1)	.A1-4	Societies. Associations. Congresses For prisoners' aid associations, etc., associations devoted to prison reform , see HV8987, etc.
(2)	.A5A-Z	General works. History and policy Including documents
(3)	.A6	By region or state, A-Z
(4)	.A7-Z	By city, A-Z Under each city: .x General Including documents .x2 Institutions. By name, A-Z

By region or country

The world

9441 Official reports of commissions, etc.

9443 Nonofficial

United States

Societies, associations, see HV8987

Documents, including reports, see HV7245+, Criminal statistics; HV7561+, Police; HV8311+, Prison reports

9456 Congresses. Conventions

9461 Collected works (nonserial)

9463 Directories

1/ For Table V, see pp. 135-144. Add country number in table to 9300

Penology
By region or country
United States - Continued
9465 Statistics of prisoners (Nonofficially)
9466 History
9468 Biography
Policy. Prison administration
9469 General works
.2 Public relations
Prison reform, see HV8987
9470 Wardens. Employees
Treatises on American systems
Including federal prison system
9471 General works
9473 Official reports
Class here foreign investigations, etc.
9474 Federal prisons, A-Z
9475 By state, A-W
Under each:
.x General works
.x2 State institutions. By name A-Z
For documents and reports, see reference above HV9456
9481 By city or county, A-Z
Under each city:
.x General works
.x2 Institutions. By name, A-Z
9501-9920.5 Other regions or countries (1801-). Table IX 1/
HV9649 subdivided like HV249, English counties.
Ancient and medieval penology through 1800, see HV8508+
Under each country:

10 nos.	5 nos.	2 nos.	1 no.	
				Societies, associations, see HV8992+. Documents, including reports, see HV7315+; Criminal statistics; HV7641+, Police; HV8395+, Prison reports
(2)	(1)			Congresses. Conventions
(3)	(1.5)		.A1-5	Collected works (nonserial)
(4)	(2)			History and statistics (Nonofficial works)
(6)	(3)			Policy. Prison administration For prison reform literature, see HV8980+

1/ For Table IX, see pp. 135-144. Add country number in table to 9500

Criminology
Penology
By region or country
9501-9920.5 Other regions or countries (1801-).
Table IX 1/ - Continued
Under each country:

10 nos.	5 nos.	2 nos.	1 no.	
(7)		(1)	.A6-Z7	General works. Treatises. Including national prison systems. Official foreign investigations, etc.
(8)	(3.5)			National prisons, A-Z
(9)	(4)		.Z8	By region, state, or province, A-Z. Under each state: (1) General works (2) Institutions. By place, A-Z. For documents and reports, see reference above subdivisions (2) and (1)
(10)	(5)			By city, A-Z. Under each city: (1) General works (2) Institutions. By name, A-Z. Cf. note to subdivisions (9) and (4) above

1 For Table IX, see pp. 135-144. Add country number in table to 9500

Periodicals. Serials
1 American
.A01-9 Early to ca. 1860/70. By date of earliest issue
Including English periodicals
e. g. HX1.A11 The Economist, 1821-
.A12 New Harmony gazette, 1825- , continued as Free enquirer, Free enquirer, 3rd ser.
.A13 The Co-operative magazine, 1826-
.A14 The Crisis, 1832-
.A15 The New moral world, 1834-
.A16 The Working man's advocate, 1844-
.A17 The Moral world, 1845-
.A175 Weekly letters to the human race, 1850-
.A18 Robert Owen's journal, 1851-
.A182 Robert Owen's Rational quarterly review and journal, 1853-
.A19 Millennial gazette, 1856-
3 English
For early, to ca. 1860/70, <u>see</u> HX1
5 French
6 German
7 Italian
8 Slavic
9 Other languages, A-Z
11 Societies. Associations
e. g. Communist International, <u>see</u> .I5
.F2-5 Fabian Society
.I5 The International. Communist International
Congresses
13.A3A-Z General works
.A5-Z Individual congresses. By date
15 Collected works (nonserial)
17 Dictionaries. Encyclopedias
18 Terminology
19 Study and teaching. Schools
Cf. HX526, Socialism and education
History
21 General works
23 Biography (Collective)
Class individual biography with special period, HX26+ or with country, HX84
By period
26 Ancient
31 Medieval
Cf. HX629, Medieval communism

History
By period - Continued
Modern
36 General works
38 French revolution
19th century
39 General works
.5 Karl Marx
Cf. HB97.5, Marxian economics
PT2428.M47, Literary works
20th century
40 General works
44 1945-
Special systems and movements
Including both theory and history
Christian socialism
Cf. HN30+, Church and social problems
51 General works
54 Catholic socialism
56 Scientific socialism. Communism: Left-wing socialism, bolshevism
Cf. HX626+, Communism: Utopian socialism, communistic settlements
For historical treatment, see HX39+
By region or country, see HX81+
General works
Including theories, criticism, etc.
71 Early works to 1789. By date
Modern works, 1789-
For history and description of the communist regime in Russia, 1917- and of similar regimes in other countries, see DK, etc.
By region or country
America
80 General works
United States
81 Collections. Societies
83 History
Biography
84.A2 Collective
.A3-Z Individual, A-Z
General works
85 Early to 1840/50
86 1840/50-
87 Minor works: Fiction, satire, curiosa
89 Politics
For political parties, see JK2251+; for local, see HX91+
91 By region or state, A-Z
92 By city, A-Z

General works
Modern works, 1789-
By region or country - Continued

101-517.5 Other regions or countries. Table IX, modified 1/
Under each country:

10 nos.	5 nos.	
(1)	(1)	Societies. Collections
(3)	(2)	History
		Including biography
(4)	(3.5)	1945-
	(4)	General works. Treatises
(5)		Early to 1840/50
(6)		1840/50-
(7)	.Z5	Minor works: Fiction, satire, curiosa
(9)	.Z7	Politics
		For political parties, see JL - JQ
(10)	(5)	Local, A-Z

Note 1. For history in Russia use:
History
Including biography
312 Early to 1917
313 1917-

Note 2. For Pacific islands use:
516 General works
517 Local, A-Z

Note 3
517.5 Greenland

2 nos.	1 no.	
(1)		General
	.A1-5	Documents
	.A6A-Z	History and description
		Biography
	.A75A-Z	Collective
	.A8	Individual, A-Z
(2)	.A9-Z	Local, A-Z

1/ For Table IX, see pp. 135-144. Add country number in table to 100

General works - Continued

518 Special topics, A-Z

.C7 Self-criticism

.L4 Leadership

.R4 Revisionism

Self-criticism, <u>see</u> .C7

.S8 Strategy

519 Communism/socialism and cooperation

Cf. HD2951+, Economic history

520 Communism/socialism and architecture

521 Communism/socialism and art

522 Communism/socialism and creative ability

523 Communism/socialism and culture

526 Communism/socialism and education

Cf. HX19, Study and teaching of socialism

Communism/socialism and ethics, <u>see</u> BJ1388+

528 Communism/socialism and intellectuals

530 Communism/socialism and the law

531 Communism/socialism and literature

Cf. PN56.S66, Socialist realism in literature

533 Communism/socialism and philosophy

535 Communism/socialism and psychology

536 Communism/socialism and religion

541 Communism/socialism and science

.5 Communism/socialism and social sciences

542 Communism/socialism and society

544 Communism/socialism and trade unions

545 Communism/socialism and war

546 Communism/socialism and woman. Communism/socialism and the family

547 Communism/socialism and youth

550 Communism/socialism in relation to other topics, A-Z

.A56 Anthropology

.A7 Armies

.B8 Buddhism

.E25 Ecology

.F47 Finance

.F7 Freemasons

.G45 Geography

.I5 International relations

.I8 Islam

.J4 Jews. Judaism

.L3 Land question

.L55 Linguistics

.L7 Liquor problem

.M35 Mass media

.M4 Medicine

.M6 Middle classes

.M65 Motion pictures

.N3 Nationalism

.N66 Nonviolence

.P4 Peasantry

.P7 Property

.P77 Psychoanalysis

.T7 Trusts

Communism: Utopian socialism, collective settlements
Cf. HX56, Scientific socialism. Communism: Left-wing socialism, bolshevism

History

626 General works

628 Ancient and medieval

Modern

630 General works

632 19th-20th centuries

635 Management, organization, etc., of collective settlements

651-780.7 General works. By region or country. Table V 1/
Cf. HQ967, Free love communities
Under each country:

4 nos.	1 no.	
(1)	.A3	History
(2)		General works For works by and about Owen, see HX696.09 For works by and about Fourier, see HX704.F7+
(3)	.A38	Local (region, state, etc.), A-Z
(4)	.A4-Z	Particular communities, A-Z For works on the New Lanark establishment, see HX696.09

Communism and education, see HX526
Communism and religion, see HX536
Communism and war, see HX545

Utopias. The ideal state
Cf. PN56.U8, Utopia as a theme in literature
For Utopian novels, see P

806 General works. History

807 Religious aspects

Particular works

810 Collected works (nonserial)

811 Individual works. By date of first edition

Anarchism
Cf. HD6477, Syndicalism
HV6278, Assassination of rulers
HV8037, Provision against anarchists

821 Periodicals. Societies. Serials

History

826 General works

828 19th-20th centuries

833 General works, treatises, and advanced textbooks
For controversial works, see HX841+

841-970.7 By region or country. Table V 1/
Under each country:

4 nos.	1 no.	
(1)	.A-Z6	History
(2)		General works
(4)	.Z7	Local, A-Z

Illustrative materials, stories, fiction, etc., see class P

1/ For Table V, see pp. 134-144. Add country number in table to 650

TABLES OF GEOGRAPHICAL DIVISIONS

I	II	III	IV	V		VI	VII	VIII	IX	X
1	1-2	1-2	1-2	1	America. Western Hemisphere	1				
2	3-4	3-4	3-4	2	North America	2				
3	5-6	5-6	5-8	3-6	United States					
4	7-8	8-10	9-12		Northeastern States. New England					
5	9-10	11-13	13-16		Middle Atlantic States. Middle States					
6	11-12	14-16	17-20		Southern States					
7	13-14	17-19	21-24		Central States. Plains States					
8	15-16	21-22	25-28		Great Lakes region					
9	17-18	23-25	29-32		Mississippi Valley					
10	19-20	26-28	33-36		Southwestern States					
11	21-22	29-31	37-40		Northwestern States. Rocky Mountain region					121-130
12	23-24	32-34	41-44		Pacific States					
13	25	35	45		States, A-W					
					Including regions and counties					
14	27	38	49		Cities, A-Z					
15	29-30	41-43	53-56	7-10	Canada	10	11-20	1-10	1-10	151-160
15.25	30.25	43.25	56.25	10.25	Saint Pierre and Miquelon Islands	10.25	20.25	10.25	10.25	160.25
					Greenland, see 99.5 ...					
15.5	30.5	43.5	56.5	10.5	Latin America	11.5	20.5	10.5	10.5	160.5
16	31-32	44-46	57-60	11	Mexico	12	21-30	11-20	11-15	161-170
17	33-34	47	61-64	13	Central America	13	31-35	21-25	16-20	171-175
17.5	35-36	48	65-68	13.5	Belize. British Honduras	13.25	36-40	26-30	20.5	181-185
18	37-38	49-51	69-72	14	Costa Rica	13.5	41-50	31-40	21-25	191-195
19	39	52-54	73-74	15	Guatemala	13.75	51-60	41-50	26-30	201-205
20	40	55-56	75-76	16	Honduras	14	61-70	51-60	31-35	206-210
21	41	57-58	77-78	17	Nicaragua	14.25	71-80	61-70	36-40	216-220
22	42-43	59-60	79	18	Panama	14.5	81-85	71-75	41-45	221-225
22.5	43.5	61	80	18.5	Panama Canal Zone	14.75	86-90	76-80	45.5	226-230
23	44	62-64	81-84	19	Salvador	15	91-100	81-90	46-50	231-235

TABLES OF GEOGRAPHICAL DIVISIONS

I	II	III	IV	V		VI	VII	VIII	IX	X
					Latin America - Continued					
24	45-46	65-67	85-88	20	**West Indies. Caribbean area**	16	101-105	91-95	51	241-245
24.5	47-48	68-70	89-92	20.5	**Bahamas**	16.2	106-110	96-100	53	246-250
25	49-50	71-73	93-96	21	**Cuba**	16.3	111-120	101-110	56-60	251-260
26	51	74-75	97-98	22	**Haiti**	16.4	121-125	111-115	61	261-265
26.5	52	76	99-100	22.5	**Dominican Republic. Santo Domingo**	16.5	126-130	116-120	64	266-270
27	53-54	77-79	101-104	23	**Jamaica**	16.6	131-140	121-130	66-70	271-280
28	55-56	80-82	105-108	24	Puerto Rico	16.7	141-150	131-140	71-75	281-285
28.3	56.3	83	109	24.3	Virgin Islands of the United States	16.8	150.3	141	75.3	286-290
28.5	56.5	83.5	110	24.5	British West Indies	16.9	151	142	75.4	291
28.7	56.7	83.7	110.7	24.7	Leeward Islands	17	153	144	75.5	293
28.9	56.9	83.9	110.9	24.9	Windward Islands	17.3	154	145	75.6	294
29	57	84	111	25	Trinidad and Tobago	17.4	155	146	75.7	295
29.3	57.3	84.3	111.3	25.3	Netherlands Antilles. Dutch West Indies	17.5	156	147	75.8	296
29.5	57.5	84.5	111.5	25.5	French West Indies	17.6	157	148	75.85	297
29.7	57.7	84.7	111.7	25.7	Guadeloupe	17.7	158	149	75.9	298
29.9	57.9	85	112	25.9	Martinique	17.9	159	150	75.95	299
30	58	86-88	113-116	26	South America	18-19	161-170	151-160	76-80	301-310
31	59-60	89-91	117-120	27-30	Argentina	20-24	171-180	161-170	81-85	311-320
32	61-62	92-94	121-124	31	Bolivia	25-26	181-190	171-180	86-90	321-330
33	63-64	95-97	125-128	32-35	Brazil	28-32	191-200	181-190	91-95	331-340
34	65-66	98-100	129-132	36	Chile	33-37	201-210	191-200	96-100	341-350
35	67-68	101-103	133-136	37	Colombia	38-39	211-220	201-210	101-105	351-360
36	69-70	104-106	137-140	38	Ecuador	40-41	221-230	211-220	106-110	361-370
37	71-72	107-109	141-144	39	Guianas	42-43	231-240	221-230	111-115	371-380
37.3	72.3	109.3	144.3	39.3	Guyana. British Guiana	43.3	240.3	230.3	115.3	380.3
37.5	72.5	109.5	144.5	39.5	Surinam. Dutch Guiana	43.5	240.5	230.5	115.5	380.5
37.7	72.7	109.7	144.7	39.7	French Guiana	43.7	240.7	230.7	115.7	380.7

TABLES OF GEOGRAPHICAL DIVISIONS

I	II	III	IV	V		VI	VII	VIII	IX	X
					Latin America					
					South America - Continued					
38	73-74	110-112	145-148	40	Paraguay	44-45	241-250	231-240	116-120	381-390
39	75-76	113-115	149-152	41	Peru	46-47	251-260	241-250	121-125	391-400
40	77-78	116-118	153-156	42	Uruguay	48-49	261-270	251-260	126-130	401-410
41	79-80	119-121	157-160	43	Venezuela	50-51	271-280	261-270	131-135	411-420
42	81-82	122-124	161-164	44	Europe	52-53	281-290	271-280	136-140	421-430
42.8	82.5	124.5	164.5	44.5	European Economic Community countries	53.5	289.5	280.5	140.5	430.5
43	83-84	125-127	165-168	45	Great Britain	54-58	291-300	281-300[1]	141-150[1]	431-440
44	85-86	128-130	169-172	46	England and Wales	60-61	301-310			441-450
45	87-88	131-132	173-176	47	Scotland	62-63	311-320			451-460
45.5	88.5	132.5	176.5	47.5	Northern Ireland	63.5	320.5			460.5
46	89-90	133-135	177-180	48	Ireland. Irish Republic	64-65	321-330	300.3	150.3	461-470
47	91-92	136-138	181-184	49-52	Austria	66-67	331-340	301-320	151-160	471-480
47.3	92.3	138.3	184.3	52.3	Czechoslovakia	69.3	340.3	320.3	160.3	480.3
47.5	92.5	138.5	184.5	52.5	Hungary	69.5	340.5	320.5	160.5	480.5
47.9	92.9	138.9	184.9	52.9	Liechtenstein	69.9	340.9	320.9	160.9	480.9
48	93-94	139-141	185-188	53-56	France	70-74	341-350	321-340	161-170	481-490
48.5	94.5	141.5	188.5	56.5	Monaco	74.5	350.5	340.5	170.5	490.5
49	95-96	142-144	189-192	57-60	Germany Including West Germany	75-79	351-360	341-360	171-180	491-500
49.5	96.5	144.5	192.5	60.5	East Germany	79.5	360.5	360.5	180.5	500.5
51	99-100	148-150	197-200	62-65	Italy	85-89	371-380	371-390	186-195	511-520
51.3	100.3	150.3	200.3	65.3	San Marino	89.3	380.3	390.3	195.3	520.3
51.5	100.5	150.5	200.5	65.4	Malta	89.5	380.5	390.5	195.5	520.5
52	101-102	151-153	201-204	65.5	Benelux countries. Low countries	90-94	381-390	391-400	196-200	521-530
53	103-104	154-156	205-208	66-69	Belgium	95-99	391-400	401-410	201-205	531-540
54	105-106	157-159	209-212	70-73	Netherlands	100-104	401-410	411-420	206-210	541-550
54.5	106.5	159.5	212.5	73.5	Luxemburg	104.5	410.5	420.5	210.5	550.5

1 Class the constituent countries of Great Britain as particular localities of Great Britain in the Local, A-Z number provided

TABLES OF GEOGRAPHICAL DIVISIONS

I	II	III	IV	V		VI	VII	VIII	IX	X
					Europe - Continued					
55	107-108	160-162	213-216	74-77	Russia	105-109	411-420	421-430	211-215	551-560
55.3	108.3	162.3	217	77.3	Finland	110	421-425	431-435	215.5	561-565
55.7	108.7	162.7	218	77.7	Poland	111	426-429.5	436-439.5	215.7	566-569.5
56	109-110	163-165	219-220	78	Scandinavia	113-114	430	440	216-220	570
57	111-112	166-168	221-224	79	Denmark	115-119	431-440	441-450	221-225	571-580
58	113-114	169-171	225-228	79.5	Iceland	120-124	441-450	451-460	226-230	581-590
59	115-116	172-174	229-232	80	Norway	125-129	451-460	461-470	231-235	591-600
60	117-118	175-177	233-236	81-84	Sweden	130-134	461-470	471-480	236-240	601-610
61	119-120	178-180	237-240	85-88	Spain	135-139	471-480	481-490	241-245	611-620
61.3	120.3	180.3	240.3	88.3	Andorra	139.3	480.3	490.3	245.3	620.3
61.5	120.5	180.5	240.5	88.5	Gibraltar	139.5	480.5	490.5	245.5	620.5
62	121-122	181-183	241-244	89	Portugal	140-144	481-490	491-500	246-250	621-630
63	123-124	184-186	245-248	90	Switzerland	145-149	491-500	501-510	251-255	631-640
64	125-126	187-189	249-252	91	Balkan States	150-154	501-510	511-520	256-260	641-650
64.5	126.5	189.5	252.5	91.4	Albania	154.4	510.5	520.5	260.5	650.5
65	127-128	190-191	253-254	91.5	Bulgaria	154.5	511-520	521-530	261-265	651-660
65.5	128.5	192-193	255-256	91.6	Yugoslavia	154.6	521-525	531-535	265.5	661-665
67	131-132	196-198	261-264	91.8	Romania	154.8	531-540	541-550	271-275	671-680
67.5	132.5	198.5	264.5	91.83	Greece	154.83	540.5	550.5	275.5	680.5
68	133	199	265	91.85	Asia	154.85	541-545	551-555	276	681
68.2	133.3	200	265.5	91.9	Middle East. Near East	154.9	546	556	276.5	682
68.25	133.4	200.5	265.7	91.93	Turkey	154.93	546.5	556.5	276.7	682.5
68.3	133.5	200.6	266	91.95	Cyprus	154.95	547	557	277	683
68.35	133.7	200.9	266.5	92	Syria	155	548	558	277.5	684
68.4	133.9	201	267	92.15	Lebanon	155.15	549	559	278	685
68.45	134	201.3	267.5	92.2	Israel. Palestine	155.2	550	560	278.5	686
68.5	134.3	201.6	268	92.25	Jordan	155.25	551	561	279	687
68.55	134.5	201.9	268.5	92.3	Arabian Peninsula. Arabia	155.3	552	562	279.5	688
68.6	134.7	202	269	92.35	Saudi Arabia	155.35	553	563	280	689
68.65	134.9	202.3	269.5	92.4	Yemen (Yemen Arab Republic)	155.4	554	564	280.5	690

TABLES OF GEOGRAPHICAL DIVISIONS

I	II	III	IV	V		VI	VII	VIII	IX	X
					Asia					
					Middle East. Near East					
					Arabian Peninsula.					
					Arabia - Continued					
68.7	135	202.6	270	92.43	Yemen (People's Democratic Republic). Southern Yemen. Aden (Colony and Protectorate)	155.43	554.5	564.5	280.7	691
68.75	135.3	202.9	270.5	92.44	Oman. Muscat and Oman	155.44	555	565	281	692
68.8	135.5	203	271	92.45	United Arab Emirates. Trucial States	155.45	556	566	281.5	693
68.85	135.7	203.3	271.5	92.5	Qatar	155.5	557	567	282	694
68.9	135.9	203.6	271.6	92.52	Bahrein	155.52	558	568	283	695
68.95	136	203.9	271.7	92.53	Kuwait	155.53	559	569	284	696
69	136.3	204	272	92.55	Iraq	155.55	560	570	285	697
69.2	136.4	204.2	272.2	92.56	Iran	155.7	560.2	570.2	285.2	698
69.3	136.5	204.3	272.3	92.57	South Asia	156	560.3	570.3	285.3	700
69.6	136.6	204.6	272.6	92.6	Afghanistan	156.6	560.6	570.6	285.6	700.6
69.7	136.7	204.7	272.7	92.7	Burma	156.7	560.7	570.7	285.7	700.7
69.8	136.8	204.8	272.8	92.8	Sri Lanka. Ceylon	156.8	560.8	570.8	285.8	700.8
69.9	136.9	204.9	272.9	92.9	Nepal	156.9	560.9	570.9	285.9	700.9
71	139-140	208-210	277-280	97-100	India	160-164	571-580	581-590	291-295	711-720
71.3	140.3	210.3	280.3	100.3	Bhutan	164.3	580.3	590.3	295.3	720.3
71.5	140.5	210.5	280.5	100.5	Pakistan	164.5	580.5	590.5	295.5	720.5
71.6	140.6	210.6	280.6	100.6	Bangladesh	164.55	580.6	590.6	295.6	720.6
72	141-142	211-213	281-284	101	Southeast Asia. Indochina Including French Indochina	164.6	580.8	590.8	295.8	721-730
					Burma, <u>see</u> 69.7 ...					
73.3	144.3	216.3	288.3	102.3	Cambodia	164.63	590.3	600.3	300.3	740.3
73.4	144.4	216.4	288.4	102.4	Laos	164.64	590.4	600.4	300.4	740.4

I	II	III	IV	V		VI	VII	VIII	IX	X
					Asia					
					Southeast Asia.					
					Indochina - Continued					
73.5	144.5	216.5	288.5	102.5	Vietnam	164.65	590.5	600.5	300.5	740.5
73.55	144.55	216.55	288.55	102.55	Thailand	164.655	590.55	600.55	300.55	740.55
73.6	144.6	216.6	288.6	102.6	Malaysia. Malaya	164.66	590.6	600.6	300.6	740.6
74	145	217	289	103	Singapore	164.67	590.67	600.67	300.67	741
74.3	146.3	218.3	290	103.3	Brunei	164.68	590.68	600.68	300.68	742
75	147-148	220-222	293-296	104	Indonesia	164.7	591-600	601-610	301-305	751-760
76	149-150	223-225	297-300	105	Philippine Islands	164.8	601-610	611-620	306-310	761-770
76.5	150.5	225.5	300.5	106	East Asia. Far East	164.9	610.5	620.5	310.5	770.5
77	151-152	226-227	301-304	107	Japan	165-166	611-620	621-630	311-315	771-780
77.5	152.5	228	304.5	108	Korea Including South Korea	167	620.5	630.5	315.5	780.5
77.6	152.6	228.6	304.6	108.6	North Korea (Democratic People's Republic)	167.6	620.6	630.6	315.6	780.6
77.8	152.8	229	305	109	Outer Mongolia. Mongolian People's Republic	168	620.8	630.8	315.8	780.8
78	154	230	306	110	China	169	621-630	631-640	316-320	781-790
79	155	231	307	111	Macao	170	631-635	641-645	321-325	791-795
80	156	232	308	112	Taiwan. Formosa	171	636-640	646-650	326-330	796-800
81	157	233	309	113	Hongkong	172	641-645	651-655	331	801-805
81.5	160	239	319	116	Arab countries (Collective)	178	656	666	334	816
81.7	160.5	240	320	116.5	Islamic countries (Collective)	179	658	668	335	818
82	161	241-243	321-324	117	Africa	180-181	661-670	671-680	336-340	821-830
82.2	161.2	244	325	118	North Africa	182	671	681	340.5	831
82.3	161.3	244.3	325.3	118.3	Morocco	182.2	672	682	341	832
82.4	161.4	244.5	325.5	118.5	Algeria	182.3	673	683	341.5	833
82.5	161.5	244.7	325.7	118.7	Tunisia	182.4	674	684	342	834
82.6	161.6	245	326	118.9	Libya	182.5	675	685	342.5	835
82.7	161.7	245.3	326.3	119	Egypt. United Arab Republic	182.6	676	686	343	836
82.8	161.8	245.5	326.5	119.3	Sudan	182.7	677	687	343.5	837

I	II	III	IV	V		VI	VII	VIII	IX	X
					Africa - Continued					
82.9	161.9	245.7	326.7	119.5	Northeast Africa	182.8	678	688	344	838
83	162	246	327	119.7	Ethiopia	182.9	679	689	344.5	839
83.2	162.2	246.3	327.3	119.9	Somalia Including British and Italian Somaliland	183	680	690	345	840
83.3	162.3	246.5	327.5	120	French Territory of the Afars and Issas	183.2	681	691	345.5	841
83.4	162.4	246.7	327.7	120.3	Southeast Africa	183.3	682	692	346	842
83.5	162.5	247	328	120.5	Kenya	183.4	683	693	346.5	843
83.6	162.6	247.3	328.3	120.7	Uganda	183.5	684	694	347	844
83.7	162.7	247.5	328.5	120.9	Rwanda	183.6	685	695	347.5	845
83.8	162.8	247.7	328.7	121	Burundi	183.7	686	696	348	846
83.9	162.9	248	329	121.3	Tanzania. Tanganyika. Zanzibar	183.8	687	697	348.5	847
84	163	248.3	329.3	121.5	Mozambique	183.9	688	698	349	848
84.2	163.2	248.5	329.5	121.7	Madagascar. Malagasy Republic	184	689	699	349.5	849
84.3	163.3	248.7	329.7	121.9	Southern Africa	184.2	690	700	350	850
84.4	163.4	249	330	122	South Africa	184.3	691	701	350.5	851
84.5	163.5	249.3	330.3	122.3	Rhodesia Including Southern Rhodesia	184.4	692	702	351	852
84.6	163.6	249.5	330.5	122.5	Zambia. Northern Rhodesia	184.5	693	703	351.5	853
84.7	163.7	249.7	330.7	122.7	Lesotho. Basutoland	184.6	694	704	352	854
84.8	163.8	250	331	122.9	Swaziland	184.7	695	705	352.5	855
84.9	163.9	250.3	331.3	123	Botswana. Bechuanaland	184.8	696	706	353	856
85	164	250.5	331.5	123.3	Malawi. Nyasaland	184.9	697	707	353.5	857
85.2	164.2	250.7	331.7	123.5	Southwest Africa (Namibia)	185	698	708	354	858

TABLES OF GEOGRAPHICAL DIVISIONS

I	II	III	IV	V		VI	VII	VIII	IX	X
					Africa - Continued					
85.3	164.3	251	332	123.7	Central Africa. Equatorial Africa	185.2	699	709	354.5	859
85.4	164.4	251.3	332.3	123.9	Angola	185.3	700	710	355	860
85.5	164.5	251.5	332.5	124	Zaire. Congo (Democratic Republic)	185.4	701	711	355.5	861
85.6	164.6	251.7	332.7	124.3	Equatorial Guinea	185.5	702	712	356	862
85.7	164.7	252	333	124.5	São Tomé e Príncipe	185.6	703	713	356.5	863
85.8	164.8	252.3	333.3	124.7	French Equatorial Africa. French Congo	185.7	704	714	357	864
85.9	164.9	252.5	333.5	124.9	Gabon	185.8	705	715	357.5	865
86	165	252.7	333.7	125	Congo (Brazzaville). Middle Congo	185.9	706	716	358	866
86.2	165.2	253	334	125.3	Central African Republic. Ubangi-Shari	186	707	717	358.5	867
86.3	165.3	253.3	334.3	125.5	Chad	186.2	708	718	359	868
86.4	165.4	253.5	334.5	125.7	Cameroon	186.3	709	719	359.5	869
86.5	165.5	253.7	334.7	125.9	West Africa. West Coast	186.4	710	720	360	870
86.6	165.6	254	335	126	French-speaking West Africa	186.5	711	721	360.5	871
86.7	165.7	254.3	335.3	126.3	Benin. Dahomey	186.6	712	722	361	872
86.8	165.8	254.5	335.5	126.5	Togo	186.7	713	723	361.5	873
86.9	165.9	254.7	335.7	126.7	Niger	186.8	714	724	362	874
87	166	255	336	126.9	Ivory Coast	186.9	715	725	362.5	875
87.2	166.2	255.3	336.3	127	Guinea	187	716	726	363	876
87.3	166.3	255.5	336.5	127.3	Mali	187.2	717	727	363.5	877
87.4	166.4	255.7	336.7	127.5	Upper Volta	187.3	718	728	364	878
87.5	166.5	256	337	127.7	Senegal	187.4	719	729	364.5	879
87.6	166.6	256.3	337.3	127.9	Mauritania	187.5	720	730	365	880
87.7	166.7	256.5	337.5	128	Nigeria	187.6	721	731	365.5	881
87.8	166.8	256.7	337.7	128.3	Ghana	187.7	722	732	366	882
87.9	166.9	257	338	128.5	Sierra Leone	187.8	723	733	366.5	883

I	II	III	IV	V		VI	VII	VIII	IX	X
					Africa					
					West Africa					
					West Coast - Continued					
88	167	257.3	338.3	128.7	Gambia	187.9	724	734	367	884
88.2	167.2	257.5	338.5	128.8	Liberia	188	725	735	367.5	885
88.3	167.3	257.7	338.7	129	Guinea-Bissau. Portuguese Guinea	188.2	726	736	368	886
88.4	167.4	258	339	129.3	Spanish Sahara	188.3	727	737	368.5	887
					Atlantic Ocean Islands					
					Iceland, <u>see</u> 58 ...					
88.5	167.5	258.3	339.3	129.5	Azores	188.35	728	738	369	888
88.53	168	258.5	340	129.53	Bermuda	188.4	728.3	738.3	369.3	888.3
88.55	168.5	258.7	340.5	129.55	Madeira Islands	188.5	728.5	738.5	369.4	888.5
88.6	169	259	341	129.6	Canary Islands	188.6	728.7	738.7	369.5	888.7
88.63	169.5	259.3	341.5	129.63	Cape Verde Islands	188.7	728.9	738.9	369.6	888.9
88.65	170	259.5	342	129.65	St. Helena	188.8	729	739	369.7	889
88.7	170.5	259.7	342.5	129.7	Tristan da Cunha	188.9	729.3	739.3	369.8	889.3
88.73	171	260	343	129.73	Falkland Islands	189	729.5	739.5	369.9	889.5
					Indian Ocean Islands					
88.75	171.5	260.3	343.5	129.75	Maldive Islands	189.2	729.7	739.7	370	889.7
88.8	172	260.5	344	129.8	Seychelles	189.3	729.9	739.9	370.3	889.9
88.83	172.5	260.7	344.5	129.83	Comoro Islands	189.4	730	740	370.4	890
88.85	173	261	345	129.85	Mauritius	189.5	730.3	740.3	370.5	890.3
88.9	173.5	261.3	345.5	129.9	Reunión	189.6	730.5	740.5	370.6	890.5
88.93	174	261.5	346	129.93	Kerguelen Islands	189.7	730.7	740.7	370.7	890.7
89	175-176	262-264	349-352	130	Australia	190-194	731-740	741-750	371-375	891-900
97.5	192.5	288.5	384.5	130.4	New Zealand	194.6	820.5	830.5	415.5	980.5
97.55	192.55	288.55	384.55	130.43	Pacific Ocean Islands	194.7	820.7	830.7	415.6	980.7
97.6	192.6	288.6	384.6	130.45	Trust Territory of the Pacific Including Mariana, Caroline and Marshall Islands	195	821	831	415.7	981

TABLES OF GEOGRAPHICAL DIVISIONS

I	II	III	IV	V		VI	VII	VIII	IX	X
					Pacific Ocean					
					Islands - Continued					
					Hawaii, <u>see</u> 13 ...					
97.7	192.7	288.7	384.7	130.47	Guam	195.5	821.5	831.5	416	982
97.8	192.8	288.8	384.8	130.5	Papua New Guinea	196	822	832	416.5	983
98	193	289	385	130.53	Solomon Islands	196.5	823	833	416.7	984
98.3	193.3	289.3	385.3	130.55	New Caledonia	197	824	834	417	985
98.4	193.4	289.4	385.4	130.57	New Hebrides	197.5	825	835	417.5	986
98.5	193.5	289.5	385.5	130.6	Fiji Islands	198	826	836	417.7	987
98.6	193.6	289.6	385.6	130.63	Tonga	198.5	827	837	418	987.5
					Samoan Islands					
98.7	193.7	289.7	385.7	130.65	American Samoa	199	828	838	418.5	988
98.8	193.8	289.8	385.8	130.67	Western Samoa	199.5	829	839	418.7	989
99	195	292-293	389-390	130.69	Arctic regions	200	830	840	420	991-995
99.5	196	294	391	130.7	Greenland	200.5	830.5	842.5	420.5	995.5
100	197	295	393	130.9	Antarctic regions	200.7	830.7	842.7	420.7	996

TABLE OF REGIONS AND COUNTRIES IN ONE ALPHABET

The following table is usable in cases where the scheme calls for an alphabetical arrangement of regions and countries. It is provided as a guide for the best distribution of numbers. The numbers themselves sould not be regarded as fixed since it may be necessary to adjust them to conform with particular shelflist situations

Afghanistan	.A3
Albania	.A38
Algeria	.A4
Antarctic regions	.A6
Argentina	.A7
Australia	.A8
Austria	.A9
Bangladesh	.B3
Belgium	.B4
Benin	.B45
Bolivia	.B5
Brazil	.B6
Bulgaria	.B9
Burma	.B93
Canada	.C2
Caribbean area	.C27
Central America	.C35
Chile	.C5
China	.C6
Colombia	.C7
Costa Rica	.C8
Cuba	.C9
Czechoslovakia	.C95
Denmark	.D4
Dominican Republic	.D65
Ecuador	.E2
Egypt	.E3
Ethiopia	.E8
Europe	.E85
Europe, Eastern	.E852
Europe, Western	.E855
Finland	.F5
France	.F8
French Guiana	.F9
Germany	.G3
Including West Germany	
Germany, East	.G35
Ghana	.G4
Great Britain	.G7
Greece	.G8
Greenland	.G83
Guam	.G85
Guatemala	.G9
Guyana	.G95
Haiti	.H2
Honduras	.H8
Hungary	.H9
Iceland	.I2
India	.I4
Indonesia	.I5
Iran	.I7
Iraq	.I72
Ireland	.I73
Israel	.I75
Italy	.I8
Ivory Coast	.I9
Japan	.J3
Jordan	.J6
Kenya	.K4
Korea	.K8
Latin America	.L29
Lebanon	.L4
Liberia	.L7
Libya	.L75
Luxemburg	.L9
Madagascar	.M28
Malawi	.M3
Malaysia	.M4
Mexico	.M6
Morocco	.M8
Mozambique	.M85
Namibia	.N3
Netherlands	.N4
New Zealand	.N45
Nicaragua	.N5
Nigeria	.N6
Norway	.N8
Oman	.O5
Pakistan	.P18
Panama	.P2
Papua New Guinea	.P25
Paraguay	.P3
Peru	.P4
Philippines	.P6
Poland	.P7
Portugal	.P8
Puerto Rico	.P9
Romania	.R6
Russia	.R9
Salvador	.S2
Santo Domingo	.S3
Saudi Arabia	.S33
Scandinavia	.S34
Senegal	.S38
Sierra Leone	.S5
Somalia	.S58
South Africa	.S6
Soviet Union, *see* .R9	
Spain	.S7
Sri Lanka	.S72
Sudan	.S73
Surinam	.S75
Sweden	.S8
Switzerland	.S9
Syria	.S95
Taiwan	.T28
Tanzania	.T34
Thailand	.T5

Tunisia	.T8	Uruguay	.U8
Turkey	.T9	Venezuela	.V4
Uganda	.U33	Yugoslavia	.Y8
United States	.U6	Zaire	.Z28

TABLE OF REGIONS IN THE UNITED STATES

.A1-195 .... Regions

.A11 .... New England

.A115 .... Northeastern States

.A118 .... Atlantic States

.A12 .... Middle Atlantic States

.A124 .... Potomac Valley

.A127 .... Appalachian region

.A13 .... South

.A135 .... Tennessee Valley

.A137 .... Ozark Mountain region

.A14 .... North Central States
Including Great Lakes region and Old Northwest

.A145 .... Northwestern States

.A15 .... Mississippi Valley

.A16 .... Ohio Valley

.A165 .... Southwestern States

.A17 .... Western States

.A172 .... Missouri Valley

.A175 .... Pacific Southwestern States

.A18 .... Pacific coast

.A19 .... Pacific Northwestern States

.A195 .... Columbia Valley

TABLE OF STATES

I (Cutter number)		II (1 number)	III 1/ (2 numbers)
A2	Alabama	1	1
A4	Alaska	2	3
A6	Arizona	3	5
A8	Arkansas	4	7
C2	California	5	9
C6	Colorado	6	11
C8	Connecticut	7	13
D3	Delaware	9	17
D6	District of Columbia	10	19
F6	Florida	11	21
G4	Georgia	12	23
H3	Hawaii	12.5	24.5
I2	Idaho	13	25
I3	Illinois	14	27
I6	Indiana	16	31
I8	Iowa	17	33
K2	Kansas	18	35
K4	Kentucky	19	37
L8	Louisiana	20	39
M2	Maine	21	41
M3	Maryland	22	43
M4	Massachusetts	23	45
M5	Michigan	24	47
M6	Minnesota	25	49
M7	Mississippi	26	51
M8	Missouri	27	53
M9	Montana	28	55
N2	Nebraska	29	57
N3	Nevada	30	59
N4	New Hampshire	31	61
N5	New Jersey	32	63
N6	New Mexico	33	65
N7	New York	34	67
N8	North Carolina	35	69
N9	North Dakota	36	71
O3	Ohio	37	73
O5	Oklahoma	38	75
O7	Oregon	39	77
P4	Pennsylvania	40	79
R4	Rhode Island	41	81
S6	South Carolina	42	83
S8	South Dakota	43	85
T2	Tennessee	44	87
T4	Texas	45	89
U8	Utah	46	91
V5	Vermont	47	93
V8	Virginia	48	95
W2	Washington	49	97
W4	West Virginia	50	99
W6	Wisconsin	51	101
W8	Wyoming	52	103

1/ For example: Alabama, 1-2; Hawaii, 24.5-6; Wyoming, 103-104

TABLE OF CITIES IN THE UNITED STATES

City	Code
Akron	A2
Albany	A3
Allegheny	A35
Annapolis	A4
Atlanta	A7
Augusta	A9
Austin	A95
Baltimore	B2
Baton Rouge	B3
Bismarck	B63
Boise	B66
Boston	B7
Bridgeport	B78
Buffalo	B9
Cambridge	C2
Camden	C22
Charleston, S.C.	C3
Charleston, W.Va.	C32
Cheyenne	C38
Chicago	C4
Cincinnati	C5
Cleveland	C6
Columbia, S.C.	C68
Columbus	C7
Dallas	D2
Dayton	D3
Denver	D4
Des Moines	D5
Detroit	D6
Dover	D7
Dubuque	D8
Duluth	D88
Elizabeth	E4
Erie	E6
Evansville	E9
Fall River	F2
Fort Wayne	F7
Frankfort	F8
Galveston	G2
Grand Rapids	G7
Guthrie	G8
Harrisburg	H2
Hartford	H3
Helena	H4
Hoboken	H6
Holyoke	H7
Houston	H8
Indianapolis	I4
Jackson, Miss.	J2
Jacksonville	J3
Jefferson City	J4
Jersey City	J5
Kansas City	K2
Lawrence	L4
Lincoln	L65
Little Rock	L67
Los Angeles	L7
Louisville	L8
Lowell	L9
Lynn	L97
Madison	M18
Manchester	M2
Memphis	M4
Milwaukee	M5
Minneapolis	M6
Mobile	M7
Montgomery	M75
Nashville	N2
New Bedford	N3
New Britain	N33
New Haven	N37
New Orleans	N4
New York	N5
Newark	N6
Newcastle	N63
Newport	N67
Newton	N7
Norfolk	N8
Oakland	O2
Olympia	O4
Omaha	O5
Paterson	P2
Peoria	P3
Petersburg	P4
Philadelphia	P5
Pierre	P57
Pittsburgh	P6
Portland, Me.	P7
Portland, Oreg.	P8
Providence	P9
Raleigh	R2
Reading	R3
Richmond	R5
Rochester	R6
Sacramento	S12
Saginaw	S13
St. Joseph	S14
St. Louis	S2
St. Paul	S3
Salem, Mass.	S33
Salem, Oreg.	S34
Salt Lake City	S35
San Antonio	S37
San Francisco	S4
Santa Fe	S43
Savannah	S45

City	Code
Schenectady	S48
Scranton	S5
Seattle	S6
Sioux City	S62
Somerville	S69
South Bend	S72
South Omaha	S73
Spokane	S76
Springfield, Ill.	S8
Springfield, Mass.	S82
Springfield, Ohio	S83
Syracuse	S97
Tacoma	T2
Tallahassee	T3
Terre Haute	T4
Toledo	T6
Topeka	T65
Trenton	T7
Troy	T8
Utica	U8
Washington	W3
Waterbury	W4
Wheeling	W5
Wilkes-Barre	W6
Wilmington, Del.	W7
Wilmington, N.C.	W8
Worcester	W9
Yonkers	Y5
Youngstown	Y8

INDEX

F

G

J

K

Q

R

T

☆ U.S. GOVERNMENT PRINTING OFFICE : 1990 O - 266-811